SHATTERED
SHAKEN
and
STIRRED

SHATTERED
SHAKEN
and
STIRRED

**RECONNECTING WITH WHAT MATTERS MOST
AFTER LOSS AND ADVERSITY**

GILBERT AHRENS

Published by Positano Press LLC, www.positanopress.com

Jacket design and interior formatting by Anne McLaughlin, Blue Lake Design,
Dickinson, Texas.

Some names and identifying details have been changed to protect the identities of
those involved.

Library of Congress Cataloging-in-Publication Data:
Ahrens, Gilbert von der Schulenburg, 1963 –
Shattered, shaken and stirred: reconnecting with what matters most after loss and
adversity / Gilbert S. Ahrens
ISBN 978-0-9842895-1-6 (paperback)
Printed in the United States of America.

*Kim: my wife, love, partner, and inspiration to believe
far beyond what can be seen.*

Olivia: living proof that miracles happen daily.

*The One who reigns above all: the One from whom all is given
and to whom our all is deserved.*

CONTENTS

*A*T ITS CORE, THIS BOOK IS A LOVE STORY. The subject may not be love, but the object certainly is. This book is the direct result of my witnessing of incredible, spontaneous love and support from family, friends, neighbors, co-workers and complete strangers. This huge outpouring of love in action was both humbling and inspiring.

There were more people involved than I can possibly remember, and many of whom I never met and still don't know. This book is my humble gift of thanks to this incredible group of people who loved us in an unusual time of need. While this book may be the kind of gift that deserves to be left unopened (or re-gifted!), it is at least for me a demonstrable way to express my thanks collectively to many people whom I cannot adequately repay individually.

There are, of course, many people who deserve specific mention. My parents, Gil and Christine, and parents-in law, Ray and Maxine, have epitomized gracious, loving parents. My sister, Margot Hayes, and brother in-law, Greg Hudson, have proved that family and great friends need not be mutually exclusive.

Our first responder friends, Missy Leathers, Diana Williams and Sissy Deane have always been rocks. Elizabeth Bohannon, Inga Aksamit and Laureen Novak were former nurses from Marin who dispensed way more than good medicine. Words cannot express their compassion or convey my gratitude.

Ann Million, Francie Low, Kathleen Justice-Moore, Laura Schafer, Karen Moore, Teri Elniski, Betsy Conlan, Marilee Brooks, and Olga Stevko moved us beyond measure as they moved mountains on our behalf. Erin and Tom Becker took loving care of our house and dogs while we couldn't. Mike and Tara Kesecker were always there for us, and still are.

My core guy groups: New Canaan Society, The Calvary SF Friday Morning Men's Group, The Cave, Lake Buchanan Annual Retreat, and Time-Out. Their fellowship fills my tanks when I'm running on vapors.

Some of my many friends: Tom Burke, Kevin Compton, Peter Coombs, Dave Dias, Mitch Deane, Ken Doroshow, Steve Dorr, Craig Haserot, Mike Kesecker, Paul Kim, Jim Lane, Tony Low, Ian MacKinnon, Paul Mayer, Eric Metaxas, Coach Don Nava, John O'Brien, Gordon Preston, Reid Rutherford, Brian Sharp, Mitch Stevko, Mark Stuart, Galen Svanas, Ian Warburg, Peter Watkins. And Todd Brooks, who left us way too early. I am blessed and made better by each of their friendships.

My former colleagues and partners at Piper Jaffray and J.P. Morgan honored me with their commitment to integrity and service to others. They also tolerated my inconsistent performance and unpredictable demeanor after the accident. Piper Jaffray extended extraordinary compassion and continues to demonstrate how its mid-western values make it unique among investment banks. Similarly, the talent and character of the people at J.P. Morgan make it the finest investment bank in the world. I am honored that I was part of such firms.

Many people helped bring this book to life. Kim Mayer, Eric Metaxas, and Mike Moritz each contributed invaluable insights, suggestions, and encouragement that helped keep me moving when I felt most stranded. My editor, Ashley Mayer, was a complete Godsend. She took a fragmented manuscript and gave it structure, balance and a greater sense of identify. Pat Springle shared with me his wisdom and experience without which I'd still be stuck, and

Anne McLaughlin helped bring my words to life with her typesetting and artistic gifts.

Thanks also goes to Pat Metheny and his management group at Ted Kurland Associates for permission to use the song title, "Dream of The Return," for one of this book's chapters.

Any significant spiritual ideas in this book were doubtless influenced by the teachings of Tim Keller, John Ortberg, Laird Stuart, and Rick Warren. I am grateful to each of them for helping me to grow and go deeper, and to keep reconnecting with what is right and true.

Finally, my family deserves a special prize for putting up with me during this long-winded project. The writing of this book was unusually difficult and it tested and strained our family beyond normally tolerable thresholds. Nevertheless, my wife Kim continued to be lovingly and patiently supportive. Without her, I'd be a mess and this book would certainly be nonexistent. Our daughter Olivia kept me in high spirits during low points, and her joyful smile was a constant reminder of my blessings. My girls make me the luckiest man on earth.

CHAPTER ONE

BECOMING SOMEONE ELSE

The unplanned inevitable journey...

My Dear Child:

Y OU WERE WITH US, TOO, DON'T YOU REMEMBER? No, of course
not. You were too young, so you were spared the hardships
that your mother and I endured. I have not wished to deceive you...
only to protect you. But the time has now come for me to lift the veil
and show you how my world once was; in the world that I knew
where there was suffering and hardship. I want you to know these
things in case your world falls off its tracks or becomes – before
your unbelieving eyes – unexpectedly and inexplicably shattered.

We were in a devastating automobile accident, the kind we had
always thought happened to "someone else." On an otherwise beautifully clear, crisp autumn evening in 2002, while traveling outside
Denver, Colorado, our car was hit head-on by a drunk driver traveling 95 miles per hour. We had been going about 60 mph.

Yes, we survived...but barely. Over time, the physical and emotional stress and strain wore away at our ability to withstand; so we
fell down, broken. When we got back up, we looked and moved a

little differently than we had before. We thought differently and saw differently and felt differently. Not necessarily worse, just...different. We had changed and been forever transformed. Not just by our accident, but through it.

In the blink of an eye, we became someone else. We lost who we were, and our hopes and dreams of what we'd envisioned our life would be like. That life is now so long ago that it seems like a ghost. It is certainly dead. But we are not. Instead, we pierced the veil that separated the world we knew and entered one we could never have imagined.

Our adversity was not unlike many others'. The experience of loss is unique to the sufferer, and there is no way that you – or anyone else – can fully comprehend another's individual anguish. It is lonely and isolating. Nevertheless, the solitary journey of loss is ironically what we all have in common. It binds us together because, of course, that lonely road is more crowded than you can imagine. Eventually, everyone is on it...but you may not realize this until you pierce the veil.

I pray that you never experience the challenges that come from loss, adversity, or heartache. And yet, I know my prayers are futile because it is inevitable that you will. We just don't know when or how. Nevertheless, try not to be bitter because it may very well be the thing that brings you back to life. If you look hard enough, you will see that the crowded road – the one you dread most – is paved with living, healing grace.

But first, you will have to wake up.

CHAPTER TWO

DREAM OF THE RETURN

The life you once knew will depart in three...two...one...

YOUR MOTHER AND I GAZED UP AT THE MOUNTAINS as we stepped out of the Hotel Palazzo Murat after another wonderfully re-laxing lunch at our favorite restaurant. The view to our left, toward the village and the ocean, was serene and tranquil, while the view of the mountains to our right was mesmerizing.

The town of Positano rose up from the Gulf of Salerno in Italy and climbed impossibly steep mountain walls. The buildings and dwellings hung suspended from the edges of cliffs as if dangled from the strings of a heavenly puppeteer, their posture and perseverance boldly defying gravity. The very walls themselves of the buildings in Positano could tell their own stories of adversity, pain, compromise, and triumph.

This hillside town was an immense human achievement. It was captivating and yet a little ominous. Your mother and I often joked that we always needed to look up the mountain before crossing the street to make sure that those cliffside buildings weren't cascading down on the village like some surreal avalanche. We felt excited and privileged to now call this place home.

Your mother and I paused on the sidewalk in front of Palazzo Murat, taking in the views and breathing in the air that was for us so carefree. We looked up and admired the cobblestoned streets that led to our house high above town. We were fortunate to have a home that offered a sweeping view of the town and ocean below. As always, we took a moment to appreciate the view from below, looking up at those buildings and the steep, winding roads that we were about to climb back.

Your mother was always the better hiker, so I let her lead the way. Living in Positano energized her like no other place, and she practically sprinted back home to tend to her flower garden. Every time we returned home from town, we rejoiced in both the journey completed and our little home that was such a sanctuary. We felt incredibly blessed.

While your mother raced ahead, I took my time admiring the ocean below, the lemon trees and wild flowers by my side, and, of course, the houses all around that seemed to be glued to the cliffs of this rugged terrain. I loved the smell of the ocean air and the feel of the cobblestones under my feet. I loved feeling the uniqueness of each cobblestone and how the uneven roughness of so many combined to make up the timeless character of this town we lived in. I thought about the steep hills and the effort it must have taken to create the roads and lay the stones I walked on. Those guys had some serious determination. I wondered if they worked as free men for hire, or as slaves. Either way, they had courage and tenacity; and they produced a functional work of art. This walk home always put me in a reflective mood, especially after a good lunch with wine.

When I finally arrived at our house, I was ready for a nap. The wine at lunch, the heat of the day, and the strenuous walk up the hill all conspired to make a mid-day snooze an absolute necessity.

Our back patio was in an olive grove and offered the perfect place for a little slumber. I rolled onto the reclining chair, closed my eyes, and took in a big breath of the fragrant air. My mouth salivated and relived my meal at Palazzo Murat as I again savored each of the seafood, wine, coffee, and gelato. Such a meal, if possible, could be better only in heaven.

It seemed like we were living there, in heaven, I thought, as I was about to doze off. Your mother and I were both content; for good reason, I reflected in my state of semi-slumber. We lived in Positano, and you had just turned seven years old, were doing great in school, and seemed to be everybody's best friend. We had always considered you a blessing and you had certainly brought immeasurable joy to our family. And, thank God, we had our health. I let those good feelings ride and carry me into a blissful, deep sleep.

The tart fragrance of lemons pierced the gentle air, subdued by the essence from the ancient twisted bark of olive trees. Both aromas were carried to me on an invisible carpet of dirt that was subtle, yet thick, in the reassurance of eternal agelessness. This tantalizing bouquet of citrus, wood, and earth was unique to our adopted home in Italy.

As my nose came alive, I thought I should get up and check on your mother, as I hadn't seen her since our walk home. How long ago was that? Certainly hours, but it seems like ages ago. I tried to lift myself out of the chair I was lying on.

Somehow, for whatever reason, I couldn't move. I couldn't even lift my head, which felt like it was being pulled further and deeper into my chair by an invisible force that was unbearable and unrelenting. I felt too weak to resist so I didn't fight it too hard, especially when I was so tired. I figured I had earned a few extra minutes and this particular moment, lying here in our garden, was enjoyable – except for feeling like my head was in a vice. Giving in was easier than fighting, and the extra pull beyond gravity felt strangely comforting.

I felt unnaturally relaxed as I chose to enjoy this feeling and not question this new strangeness. Life was good, and this moment was wonderful. The air outside was warm and cozy, and I felt some assurance that your mother was somewhere close by, probably pruning her roses and getting pricked by thorns, as usual. Life was indeed good and worth savoring for a few extra moments.

But the peculiar feeling returned, and I realized I needed to get up. I tried again to get my mind awake and snap out of my sleepiness. I attempted again to pull myself out of my chair, but I still couldn't do it.

Wow, I must be really tired, I thought, though not quite trusting that belief. What time is it, really? Have I overslept? I searched for a clock somewhere and my heart skipped a beat when I realized that I couldn't open my eyes. I thought I was awake – or at least somewhat aware – but now I couldn't make sense of where I was. The world was opaque, a cloudy, milky fog.

Suddenly the throbbing kicked in and took control of all of my senses. It began as a dull, blunt pounding metronome that quickly changed into sharp, searing clasps of pain, as if my head were attached to the rim of a flat tire running over cobblestone streets.

Then, just as I thought the pain would intensify, it changed. Suddenly, I could not feel the pain so much as hear it. A herd of elephants danced inside my head around my brain.

Thankfully, the elephants soon departed, but they were replaced by a faint smell that was oddly familiar. Though distant, I could tell that it wasn't a fragrance I liked. I could tell that it had nothing to do with citrus or wood or earth. This was something foreign and definitely not welcome.

Without further notice, the smell of ammonia rushed into my brain as if swept by a tornado through an open door. Ammonia meant that something wasn't right, and I felt both unnerved and nauseated. My heart skipped another beat as I tried to move...but could not. I then attempted to open my eyes, but my eyelids were immoveable, as if stapled shut.

I summoned all my strength to escape these strange assaults on my senses – the throbbing, pounding pain and the stinging smell of ammonia. I didn't want to leave my wonderful dream, but the ammonia in my face demanded that I do so. I fought off the ammonia and tried to deny the awful intrusion by sending myself back to my olive grove. Oohhh, I thought, it was such a good dream. And I'm still so tired. Let me go back there...just for a little while.

The ammonia came again, in an unwelcome, horrible wave. It folded over me, and I tumbled down cobblestoned streets in an inescapable and awful awareness that we were not in Positano. We never had been. The ammonia slapped again against my forehead. Reluctantly, I disconnected from my dream and opened my eyes.

The world then awoke within me, and it was not the world I had just been in. We were not in Positano, and you were not seven – you were not even yet one. Your mother and I had always dreamed of moving to Positano, but it had never happened. Now, that dream was over. That world had never existed except through our hopes and dreams, and I now realized with harsh clarity that, in all likelihood, that world now never would. In the blink of an eye, our world stopped in its tracks – life as we knew it was over. Not dead, just changed forever. We were derailed by an involuntary track change that had thrown us into a ditch not of our own digging.

CHAPTER THREE

MEETING THE DRAGON

Nothing clarifies the mind like the prospect of imminent death.

YOU, YOUR MOTHER, AUNT MARGOT, AND I were driving on a four-lane, undivided highway that deserved to have a median divider, given the volume and speed of traffic. Heading toward Denver, we were traveling with the masses, many perhaps destined for a night on the town. The headlights and taillights were like thousands of threads that formed white and red ribbons, which billowed slowly and effortlessly along the contours of the gentle mounds of the Rocky Mountain foothills.

Suddenly, I noticed a slight change in the white ribbon, as if a single thread had torn itself loose from the fabric. The ripple was subtle at first, but the slight aberration somehow caught my eye. The thread broke free, causing the ribbon to rip apart. My eyes were riveted on this wild single thread that transmitted a penetrating and fiery light.

The intensity of the light grew as it rushed towards us. Our car was in its path, and we were trapped, bound tightly within our ribbon. Flames grew out of this fiber as it transmogrified into a ghastly dragon. Its eyes were not the benign white of the ribbon but, rather, a jaundiced and menacing yellow: the eyes of a starved and angry beast. The Dragon's eyes told me that we were its target. We were not a deliberate target but, rather, a random and convenient opportunity to unleash its destructive power.

Yet, in that instant when I realized that sudden impact was inevitable, that certainty illuminated the world with bright, perfect clarity. It was eerily calming, given the chaos that I knew was about to unfold. Time was captured briefly and hung suspended as the physical world played out in slow motion, in a deliberate and ominously predictable dance.

It was a dance without music or any sound at all. The air was heavy with the expectant silence of…inevitability. The temporary dancers in this mute drama – not recruits, but certainly not volunteers –performed without audition or rehearsal, knowing that we were powerless to alter the script. As I watched this slow-moving pantomime, I was able to detach myself from it, hovering above with a full view of all the characters, including myself.

I knew that I was powerless to alter the Dragon's course. It felt the helplessness of a nightmare – I wanted to scream – needed to scream – but could not. I opened my mouth…but nothing came out. My eyes were the only things I could move in my entire body. Even my heart seemed to have stopped, waiting to see whether it should resume beating or succumb to the oncoming blast.

My mind, however, had time for what it needed to do. It wasn't much time, based on how we normally perceive and measure time and space, but I had just enough time for the only appropriate reaction. Somehow, I was able to say, "Oh no…God save us."

He did. And He does.

It was like a bomb had gone off. Our car came to a dead stop in an unnaturally short amount of time. There was a sickening "thud," much like the sound you experience when you hit your forehead with the butt of your hand, only worse. It was not a "bang" that comes from an explosion nearby. The "thud" meant that we were in the explosion; we were part of it. And it became part of us. Forever.

My ears rang, and my nose came alive with the hideous, unnatural smell of compressed metal. When I opened my eyes, I was dizzy and distorted. I inhaled a nauseating mix of blood and sulfur: the blood was mine, courtesy of the blown-out windshield and driver-side window; the sulfur was courtesy of the airbag that had, gratefully, deployed. I then smelled gasoline leaking from the deveined wreckage. The smell of gas was disconcerting as we were trapped in our mangled car, but it was familiar and made me realize that I was alive.

You, my daughter, were crying…which was a good sign. I heard your Aunt Margot, seated in the passenger's seat, struggle to get out of the car and finally kick her door open. She told me she was going to check on you. "Olivia's okay, but Kim is hurt," she said. I heard your mother moaning, and realized that she was more than just "hurt." Margot got you out of your infant car seat but couldn't do much for your mother.

I put my right arm behind the seat and tried to reach for your mother. I found one of her arms, which was flailing away. "Easy, Sweetie," I said. "I am with you, and God is with us. Hang in there. Help is coming. God is here. I can feel Him." I was physically unable to do much else, but quickly realized my two-part mission: 1) pray like crazy; and 2) make sure that anyone who might be coming to help us knew about your mother's potentially fatal allergic reaction to morphine.

A voice came yelling from behind, out of the darkness. "Are you okay?! Is everybody all right?!" A man rushed to the backseat. He told me that his name was John; that he had seen the accident from a few cars back and knew we would need help.

"She's really hurt," he said, referring to your mother. I asked him if he would mind if we prayed together. He did not, so we did. I then told John about your mother's morphine allergy. I was determined to get her out of this alive – and that included making sure she wasn't killed by a common painkiller.

I was powerless to help her. I couldn't move or even turn around because my feet were caught somewhere in the floorboard and my chest was held tight by the steering wheel. I started to feel a sickening mixture of bile, rage, and helplessness brewing in the pit in my stomach.

I wiped some blood from my face and looked around, outside the car. It was ghastly. Thirty feet in front of me was a heap of twisted metal. Just moments before, it had been a car. Now, it was…what?! Half a car?! What happened to the other half? My eyes scanned the horizon, over all the glass and debris on the asphalt. Then my mind raced beyond redline, unable to find a gear and fully engage with any of the information it was being fed.

What a mess…debris everywhere…half a car…blood over everything…that over there?…looked like a body…clearly dead…so much blood…no legs…oh no, it's just a torso. I saw him alive, I swear, right before impact…he looked right at me…terrified, screaming, "Nooooooo!" Eyes open even wider. Now just 15 feet away…about as dead as dead can be. Thankfully quick…hopefully at peace.

I wondered if God spoke to him? Did he cry out to God while flying through his windshield? Did he hit our car? Our windshield? Did he suffer? What killed him: hitting his head or being cut in half? Was he already dead when he lost his legs? Oh God, have mercy on his soul. Have mercy on mine. Oh, his poor parents. Lord, please comfort them.

The wretched thought onslaught was mercifully interrupted by a blinding flashlight suddenly shining in my eyes. "Are you all right?" asked a voice.

"Yeah, I'm okay," I responded, "but my wife in back is hurt badly. I can't really move to help her."

The police officer introduced himself: "I'm Officer Randy Hernandez. Help is on the way." He shined his flashlight down on my trapped foot and then back on your mother. Officer Hernandez then held my other hand, and he, John, and I all prayed together.

I heard a helicopter approaching and land nearby. "Is that for Kim?" I asked Officer Hernandez.

"No," he said, "we can't get her out of the car. The helicopter is for another victim."

"*Come on!*" I pleaded. "Can't you just pull her out of the other back door?! It's open; John came right in that way!"

"The problem," Officer Hernandez calmly told me, "is that your wife is very badly injured. Her body is in an awkward position and we can't risk pulling her out of that other door. It might further complicate her injuries. Don't worry," he assured me, "we'll get her out soon."

Another officer approached us and said that all the other emergency helicopters were at other accident scenes. We would have to wait for an ambulance, of which there was a shortage as well.

"Bad night," Officer Hernandez said, consolingly.

"Tell me about it," I replied, more sarcastically than I had intended.

We were eventually pried loose by the "jaws of life" from our smoking car, were stabilized and strapped down onto stretchers, and then practically thrown into an ambulance. Your mother was completely unresponsive to voice commands but moaning in shock and pain. We rode together in the same ambulance, but I couldn't see her because our heads were stabilized in neck braces. I kept telling the paramedics about your mother's morphine allergy and kept asking them about her condition. The revolting pit in my stomach returned when the response that came back, along with an obvious avoidance of eye contact, was "not good."

The brutally long ambulance ride ended with an abrupt flurry of activity when your mother and I were rushed into a large emergency room. Someone swung a large curtain in between your mother and me, preventing me from seeing her. But I could hear her. And her agonizing moans caused the bile in my stomach to churn in torment. It expanded as the absence of action grew longer and louder. I was expecting to hear someone issue assertive commands followed by action and coordinated movement. The lack of such noise was disturbing.

I was then startled by a young and brash ER doctor who swooped into my "room" and engaged the paramedics in a heated debate about whether to operate on my foot in an attempt to repair it or to simply amputate it. I raised my hand and, somewhat sarcastically, encouraged the doctor to give it his best shot.

By the time this was settled, I finally heard commotion from the next room and learned that this particular hospital wasn't equipped to deal with your mother's injuries. She needed to be heli-ported to another hospital. At least there was some action, and at last, she was moving in the direction of surgery. The sound of her suffering was killing me.

&

I awoke the next morning in the hospital. It didn't take long for everything to come rushing back. When I opened my eyes, I was greeted by your grandfather and uncles Paul and Craig. A physician and a police officer were also hovering nearby. Collectively, they informed me of all that had transpired, all of which I already knew but hoped had been a bad dream. They said it was a miracle that we had all survived, given the speed of impact and since it had been a head-on collision. They confirmed that one individual had indeed died: the person I had seen lying facedown in the road. He was only 18 years old, the same age as the driver who hit us. I later learned that they had been best friends.

Sadly, the accident was no dream, despite my best efforts to somehow replace it with a vision of what life was supposed to look like down the road. That dream was shattered that night, on a road outside Denver. Oh God, I thought, this was no nightmare; this was real. Then I thanked God for saving us. I somehow knew that you, your mother, and Margot were all right. How we all survived is hard for me to believe. It defies logic – which, of course, is sensible only when viewed from the perspective that miracles cannot be explained in human terms, only in divine ones.

During that brief moment right before the collision, when my mind escaped the horror of inevitability and journeyed to a place where time slowed down and I could sense a greater force, I had enough time to ask God to save us. In that instant, right before impact, I knew – with absolute certainty – that God was present. I knew He was there with us not so much because I could hear Him or see Him, but because I could *feel* Him. He was there with us. And, right before impact, I could feel Him say, "This is going to be bad, but don't worry. I am with you."

God was there when we needed Him. I could not have imagined how much more we would need Him going forward.

CHAPTER FOUR

Getting Acquainted

Some stars shine brighter from a distance.

We had traveled to Denver to take part in a family reunion of sorts: Your uncle, Barry, was getting married. A wedding always reunited friends and family, but Barry's was particularly noteworthy because most of us had thought he would remain a perpetual bachelor. It also symbolized Barry's reconnection with the family after being disconnected for several years. We wanted to be part of the welcoming committee and your mother was especially supportive of my desire to reconnect with my cousin, with whom I had once been so close. Your mother and I also viewed this as an opportunity to conveniently introduce you to a majority of my clan in one concentrated weekend. We were proud parents and loved showing you off to anyone and everyone.

Barry and I had been very close as kids. We lived less than a mile apart in a small New England town. Neither of us had brothers, so we assumed that role for each other. I generally looked up to him because he was a few years older...and taller. Whereas I was the oldest in my family, Barry was the youngest; he had the combined benefit of both years and accumulated experiences passed down from his sisters. I was young and naïve while he was older, wiser, and, in my eyes, much cooler.

Even in later years, and especially in high school, I was always in Barry's shadow. He seemed naturally gifted; everything was easy or effortless for him. He was good-looking and charming, and made friends quickly and easily. He didn't just have a girlfriend; rather, he always had a flock of girls around him. All of his friends were also good-looking, many of them from very wealthy families. I marveled at his easy-going, effortless manner and was a little jealous of his ability to gracefully coast through life.

In my world, college was often a natural dividing point. Like many friends, he went to one college, and I went to another. From then on, we kept drifting further apart. I would add a new friend here and there and delighted in getting to know that person. I would occasionally hear stories of Barry's expanded network of friends, which now included people who made a point of flying over towns like the one we grew up in. Barry was hanging out with serious celebrities. And I still had a hard time getting a date. I couldn't keep up in that world...I wouldn't even be allowed through the back door. I didn't need the torment of comparing myself to someone whose shadow was being cast by the lights of Broadway and Hollywood.

Although several years had slipped by without much thought of Barry, I rejoiced when I learned of his wedding. To me, this was a sign that Barry was settling down and moving beyond the glitz and glam that so easily embraced him. Perhaps it wasn't as fulfilling for him as it had been when we were younger. Perhaps he couldn't keep up with that lifestyle or, better yet, didn't want to. Perhaps he was becoming like me...like the rest of us. Barry's wedding symbolized his reemergence in the family. He was my Prodigal Cousin, and I was thrilled to reconnect with him after such a long absence.

Your mother and I – with you in tow – were leaving San Francisco in high spirits. As we boarded our flight to Denver, your mother maneuvered onto the plane gingerly. She was still sore and weak from her C-section, which meant that I was carrying the bulk of our carry-on cargo: all the essentials for traveling with a newborn, plus my briefcase, and your mother's book bag. I had no idea, of course, that the baggage we'd return home with would be of an entirely different nature.

We picked up our rental car in Denver and I dutifully set out to secure your car seat. I was unacquainted with that particular car model and very unfamiliar with how to secure the child's safety seat. I did an adequate job and it felt secure, but I was still uneasy. In an uncharacteristic move – perhaps because I was a little out of my skin as a new father, – I walked back into the rental office and asked for car seat anchors. As it turned out, it was a good move. It probably spared you from the Dragon.

It was a Friday night, and the Colorado air was cool and crisp, which heightened my sense of excitement. I hustled us to the rehearsal dinner so I could proudly introduce you to all the members of my family. I constantly referred to you as our "Munchkin," and was equally fond of all the variations of your nickname: "Munch," "Munchie," "the Munch." On this particular Friday night, I could not have been happier. I was also proud. I know it's not appropriate or polite to be boastful, but I thought my girls were worthy.

Thankfully, the wedding was in the afternoon the next day. Your mother and you, our Munchie, both needed your beauty rest, and I was not about to deprive you of a few hours of much-needed sleep. I needed some rest as well, but I had a strange relationship with sleep. More often than not, the times I needed sleep the most were when I most wanted to be awake. I didn't fear sleep (though I would come to find it terrifying later on); I just enjoyed being awake more.

Barry's wedding day was beautiful, a bonus since both the ceremony and the reception were outdoors. Before traveling to the wedding site, however, your mother and I managed to watch on television the first half of the Texas-Oklahoma football game. For those who had attended the University of Texas (as did your mother and her parents, grandparents, great-grandparents...back five generations), there was no rivalry that compared to that with Oklahoma University on the gridiron. Imagine Harvard-Yale, Cal. Berkeley-Stanford, Red Sox-Yankees, Giants-Dodgers, Ali-Frazier, Beatles-Stones, all rolled up into one...it still could not approximate the severity or intensity of the UT-OU rivalry.

I learned early on in our marriage that there are some things that women bring with them that cannot be encroached upon. These things are surrounded by a 20-foot barbed-wire fence, bejeweled with elephant-killing electromagnetic torpedoes, set to obliterate anyone within a mile of its perimeter. A single, slightly raised, questioning eyebrow would incite menacing death rays from the eyes of a spouse who was normally so gentle and sweet. Thankfully, your mother had only one such sacred cow. In her case, it was actually a steer, one that went by the name "BEVO," the mighty mascot of the University of Texas and the embodiment of Longhorn Football.

I grew up in a small town in the small state of Connecticut and could not appreciate the importance of football to those who lived in bigger states. Growing up where I did, I had some impression that Texans came from another planet, although I think your mother was the first Texan I had ever met. Thank God that I met her in San Francisco, because that city is about the only place in the world where a Connecticut Yankee like me could meet a Texan without running for the hills. Within about a minute of meeting your mother, I learned that she went to UT and loved football. I thought this was cute. I was soon corrected: this was serious.

Fortunately, instead of merely tolerating her football fetish, I began to embrace it. I started to admire the tradition that bound all of these people from this gigantic state of Texas and enormous institution of UT. The vehicle that connected them was football, but that connectedness transcended the game and permeated their lives to mold their collective identities. I found it endearing and a little bit infectious. I summoned the courage to throw my guarded, Yankee-born caution to the wind and became a fanatical UT football fan as well. Not long thereafter, your mother anointed me an "Honorary Longhorn." It was one of my proudest moments.

Therefore, prior to your Uncle Barry's wedding, we needed to catch as much of the UT-OU game as possible. The season had been a bit of a disappointment, but beating OU would rectify everything and possibly earn us (see, I'm now one of *them*) a spot in a decent Bowl game. OU was very good that year, perhaps one of their best teams ever, but losing to them would still be miserable. We caught the early part of the game in our hotel room as we got dressed. You, little Munchie, also seemed to like it. We knew that the wedding was going to conflict with the end of the game, so we brought a small, hand-held portable television to the wedding. Like I explained, don't try to scale the 20-foot-high fence.

We arrived at the wedding site a little early. It was outdoors and marvelously sunny, which killed the picture quality on our tiny TV screen. We had to settle for "listen-only" mode instead. We sat in the last row of seats because we wanted to be respectful: we had an infant who might make sudden loud noises…and we had a football game that might likewise evoke sudden, even louder noises. Sadly, the Longhorns lost (badly) to OU. Fortunately, the game ended before the wedding began, thereby saving us from potential conflict and embarrassment.

It was a wonderful wedding, as most unions are. The reception moved to an adjacent party tent, and the usual festivities commenced. Your mother and I continued to show you off and reconnect with family and friends, some of whom I hadn't seen in years. There were lots of pictures and hugging and mugging amidst the dinner, toasts, and wedding cake.

Before the evening started to wear on, you needed a diaper change. Then you needed to be fed. Then you needed another diaper change. Before we knew it, you needed to be fed again. This was our signal to make our exit. We had stayed long enough and were tired from another night's sleep interrupted by the cries of a hungry infant. We said some quick good-byes and made our escape. Your Aunt Margot seized the opportunity to hitch a ride with us back to the hotel.

Ten minutes later, we confronted the Dragon. Your meal had to wait way beyond our expectations. And your mother would never again successfully nurse you, her only child.

CHAPTER FIVE

IN REPAIR

❧

Real heroes are those that come to you...
you shouldn't have to go to them.

AN AMBULANCE DROVE ME THE NEXT DAY to St. Anthony Hospital in order to be in the same hospital as your mother. My parents greeted me and tried to prepare me. "Kim's very badly hurt," they said. "She's got tubes all over the place, including one in her mouth, so she can't talk." I was beginning to remember why I hated hospitals. "She shattered her leg and broke her neck," they continued. I became light-headed, and the rest of their words were but meaningless garbled sounds, accompanied by concerned gestures. Somewhere the word "coma" jumped through the clutter.

Your mother was in the Surgical Intensive Care Unit (SICU). When we approached the waiting room, I saw your other grandmother, Maxine. She had been crying and tried to pull herself together when she saw me coming.

"Oh, Gil..." she cried, giving me a big hug. "How are you?"

"How's Kim?" I answered.

"Oh, I don't know. I don't know. It's so horrible."

Your grandfather Ray came over and shook my hand and looked me squarely in the eyes. Then, in the way that only a quiet, strong gentleman from West Texas can, he said, "The doctors think that Kim might be paralyzed." I went numb. *What does that mean? What do we do?* My brain tried to search for some kind of meaning to attach to this, but found nothing. I was utterly clueless.

When I rolled into her room, my cluelessness was overwhelmed by her helplessness. My heart sank as I saw her lying in her hospital bed, with more tubes and machines connected to her than I thought possible. It was surreal. I couldn't tell if she was really alive or if all those machines were humming, pumping, and gyrating on their own. They had flashing lights and little beeps and spewed forth reams of paper emblazoned with a cryptographic code. It looked like the bizarre combination of a control room in a nuclear reactor and a Wall Street trading floor.

I saw your mother move her arm and I got excited. "That's a great sign, right?!" I asked the physician standing on the opposite side of your mother's bed.

"Not really," he replied. "That's just an involuntary movement. Her body is in a state of shock right now." My heart sank again. "We won't know how bad it is for a few more days still. Right now, I'm not predicting that she'll get back the use of her arms." My heart sank even deeper. *Oh my God. I can't believe it. I just can't believe it.*

I reached over the railing of your mother's bed and held on to a part of her arm that was free of tubes. I prayed for God to help her. To help us. I prayed for God to be with *us.* Then I remembered the voice that I had felt more than heard in the car on that awful night from a few hours before but that had seemed like a century ago:

"I am with you."

I stayed with your mother for I don't know how long. It could never have been long enough. I couldn't stand the thought of her being alone, and I would feel unbelievably guilty if I left her side.

I hadn't been able to protect her in the car, and I was sickened by the notion that she might feel abandoned as she lay helpless in her hospital bed.

YAFFE HOUSE

All of your grandparents were frantic with worry and grief. My parents had been at Barry's wedding, so they at least had the benefit of being on location. Your mother's parents, however, living in Texas, were awakened by a phone call at 3:00 AM, advising them to take the earliest flight to Denver to be near their critically injured daughter.

At some point on Sunday afternoon, a day after the accident, a volunteer from the Police Department greeted your grandparents in the hospital. Apparently, her title was "Victim's Advocate." I had no idea just how much I would come to appreciate and celebrate this kind of service that works on behalf of so many disempowered, voiceless victims. This wonderful person arranged for your grandparents to take up residence at a place called "Yaffe House." It was a house run and managed by Catholic nuns with the sole purpose of providing rest and comfort to those who had loved ones in critical care situations at the nearby hospital.

Yaffe House was a Godsend, like a port to a lost ship in a storm. You, your grandparents, and Margot all bunkered in at Yaffe House while your mother and I stayed on separate wings in the hospital. We were all close by, but still painfully disconnected.

Yaffe House was a short distance from the hospital, so the entire gang would pack up to come see your mother and me for hours at a time. I would shuttle up and down between my room and your mother's, flying awkwardly down the hallways in my wheelchair.

INTAKES AND OUT-TAKES

Along our long, crazy journey, I wrote correspondences to family and friends to keep them updated on our situation. These writings allowed me to express my joy and gratefulness, as well as my occasional anger, frustration, and exasperation. At various points, I tried to infuse things with some levity or even an injection of humor. In hindsight, I now realize that these attempts were mostly sad, sorry, woefully inept, or just plain incomprehensible. No matter: they at least provided some temporary amusement or distraction for their author (me). Even if self-induced, being easily amused helps prevent the heart from hardening.

The sad truth, however, is that I took great pride in my humor, which a Christian critic would consider to be a double sin, given the quality of my humor. I make no apologies if my humor fails to find your funny bone. If you don't understand it, then you must be too serious, too smart, or too tall. However, you may need to sink down to my level in order to appreciate the simple elegance of my silliness. Fear not: I won't take you down in the gutter…but you can't be afraid to get a little dirty. It might even require a leap of faith, of sorts. All good things do: God, marriage, golf, investing, democracy, sunscreen, Jazz music, Beaujolais Nouveau, and eating raw oysters, to name a few. Of course, it is not the leap that most of us fear. It's the landing.

My writings were illustrative of heightened and scrambled emotions that were then beyond the reach of my conscious mind. I was on a "survivor's high" and just happy that we were all alive. My correspondences allowed me to vent some hot air and release my jangled nerves. Also, I needed to keep busy to avoid going crazy.

OCT 18, 2002

I cannot adequately give thanks enough for all the incredibly thoughtful and generous offers of support that have come pouring in. I feel truly blessed to be alive and surrounded by such a generous abundance of faith, family and friends. The loving emails, faxes and letters bring me to my knees and fill my heart with humble gratitude that I am connected with such wonderful people.

Kim's condition is very serious, but thankfully, no longer life threatening. She has made remarkable improvements since those first few days early last week, but she still has no sensitivity below her chest due to the severe spinal cord injury she incurred. She can now move her eyes, mouth, arms, and hands and I remain optimistic that her momentum and her fighting spirit (as a full-blooded Texan!), combined with a huge network of prayers, will quickly progress to her lower extremities.

What happens next is still a bit unclear. I was discharged yesterday from St. Anthony Hospital but will return on Tuesday for yet another operation on my right foot, which was crushed in the accident. My new nickname is "spike" due to all the rods sticking out of my foot. They're like Frankenstein-inspired stabilizer bars.

Sadly, rehab for Kim will be quite long and, I daresay, with uncertain results, thus very stressful. I feel almost overwhelmed by all variables that need to be addressed before I can start to envision the long-term scenario. But it's critical to stay focused on the present and, right now, the bottom line is that my wife, sister, and four-week old daughter are all alive, and we're going to reconstruct our lives with faith, gusto, and enthusiasm.

OCT 19, 2002

Yesterday was great. Specifically, Kim had more moments of incredible advancement. Her sense of awareness and attentiveness was greater than ever and her arm and hand movement has really improved. She could scratch her nose and she was clawing at the ventilator tubes in her mouth, obviously very annoyed at their presence and trying to remove them herself. That's our Kim!!! She was also able to sit up in a special wheel chair for a of couple hours. Kim has always been a traveler so this was another great sign that the hospital staff was encouraging us to get out.

We went back later in the day to see Kim again. For the first time since the accident, we were able to place Olivia on her mother's chest. Kim wrapped her arms around her daughter in the most loving and contented way. It should have been difficult and clumsy for Kim, given her injuries and the countless tubes and wires attached to her body. But she made it look effortless and totally natural. It was truly one of the most wonderful and beautiful things I've ever seen. And there was not a dry eye in the house.

I feel incredibly blessed to be alive and know that God was with Kim, Olivia, Margot, and me in the car that night. I am also blessed to have the kind of faith, family, and friends that have surrounded us with such unabashed abundance during these past few days. We will need all of it going forward, but it is a wonderful feeling to be part of such incorporated and unconditional love. The generosity of spirit extended to us by others is priceless, and I know that Kim feels those prayers and is moved by them each and every day.

Thankfully, your mother began to show incredible signs of improvement – demonstrations of her strength and, more importantly, her character. A condition of extreme weakness, like your mother was in, exposes a person's true nature and disposition. I remember a couple of days in particular when your mother's spirit shined brighter than the sun.

One night later, your mother was receiving her scheduled injection of iron. I mentioned to the nurse that our sixth wedding anniversary had just passed (a day after the accident) and that, coincidentally, the traditional anniversary gifts for that year were iron and candy. I tried to add some levity to the serious mood of the injection by telling her that your mother and I both have been given enough iron (the rods and pins in our legs) and candy (of the narcotic variety) to keep us fortified well past our next anniversary.

Upon hearing this, however, your mother perked up and demanded to know if I had received my anniversary present, which she had brought to Denver. I said of course not, that too much had transpired since October 12th (the accident) and Oct 13th (our anniversary) and that I was more interested in spending time with her than locating a gift somewhere in our collected belongings in Yaffe House. But your mother was adamant. She made me promise to find that present and to bring it back with me on my next visit so that she could give it to me the way she had intended. That's your mother: gracious, and respectful of upholding traditions and honoring the love that bound us together.

The next day, we returned to visit your mother with you dressed in your Sunday best. Your mother did not remember having held you the day before, so your grandparents and I got to relive this extraordinary event. Despite the surrounding tubes and machines, both you and your mother seemed to melt into each other. You both immediately entered a state of peaceful content, and it was clear to all of us that you were being reconnected to what was right and true. Again, that was your mother: giving more to all of us than we expected or deserved.

OCT 24, 2002

This morning, the doctors removed Kim's ventilator tubes. Breathing is still difficult for her, but she is finally on her own lung-power and doing great.

Unfortunately, when Kim's breathing tube was removed from her mouth, we discovered that she was missing her two front teeth. The impact of the accident had been so severe; it's amazing that she didn't lose more than just two. Granted, relative to her other injuries, losing a couple of teeth is pretty inconsequential. Nevertheless, it was insult on top of injury. It made me concerned about what other injuries or complications we might discover.

This morning was also a time when Kim and I got to spend some quiet time together. I was able to share with her some of the cards, letters, faxes, and emails that have been flooding in from all over the place. I had read most of them many times previously so was quite surprised by the rapid erosion of my tear ducts that occurred when I re-read them aloud to Kim. Most of my tears were clearly those of joy for the realization of God's grace and the abundant love and support from so many that have touched us so deeply.

But there were moments, I confess, when the sadness of the potential loss of my wife, daughter, and sister came rushing at me without my usual filters. Also, I felt both like I had somehow let Kim down and that I had gotten off too easy. Then, seeing Kim in her bed, tough, fighting, and getting better daily...well, it took away all those fears and guilt and replaced them with the joy and hope that can come only with knowing how blessed we are.

When the physicians finally removed the ventilation tubes, they bruised her vocal cords, which made speaking yet another painful experience. A harsh, raspy whisper was all she could manage. But she needed to talk, and we discussed a range of heavy issues, many of which were the kind I never imagined having with my spouse. She wanted to know about the accident, how I was doing, and how you were holding up. And how your grandparents were doing. She reasoned they must have been horrified to see her in such a condition. She also wanted to know how close she had been to dying.

I told your mother that we were fortunate to be alive. She wondered, were we really...was *she?* Your mother began asking some very weighty questions:

"Was it worth it to go on living like this, in this broken body?" She didn't want to be a burden to me or anyone else.

"Will we make it? Will Olivia be okay? What kind of mom can I possibly be? Olivia deserves better than that." These were scary questions.

Of course, I assured your mother that everything would be all right. We would make it, and you were going to grow up and have a very special relationship with your mother. We were going to get through this together.

I answered your mother's questions with the certainty and conviction required to take a giant leap of faith. I had to leave fear and doubt behind, as they would have pulled me down early in the flight of the giant leap. My answers were persuasive because I needed to ease not just your mother's fears and concerns but my own as well.

OCT 27, 2002

HEROES

Kim and I love sports, and we've always been active in tennis, skiing, biking, whatever. We love the feeling that athletic activity gives our minds and bodies. We also love the competition, not so much to beat others, but just to push ourselves to be our best...as God wants us. We had long ago become annoyed with the popular media labeling sports stars as "Heroes," but we're even more convinced of that now, especially after the accident we had a couple of weeks ago.

Barry Bonds, Peyton Manning, Michael Jordan, Tiger Woods, Roger Federer and other titans of sports entertainment are not really heroes. They are athletes and performers who are great at what they do. They are blessed with incredible talent that does not go unrecognized. At least certainly not by the likes of Nike, ESPN, agents like IMG, and the giant media Machine. They are certainly gifted overachievers in highly demanding, competitive pursuits. Nevertheless, despite their individual accomplishments and personal sacrifices, I cannot imagine that they feel completely comfortable with being called "heroes." Certainly not after events like September 11th, or in our case, October12th. Sometimes heroes are people you do not meet until suicide bombers attack your cities or you've been hit head-on by another car while minding your own business.

Heroes are people who touch souls and save lives on a daily basis.

Heroes are bystanders, like the man named John, who rushed into the backseat of our car immediately after the accident and helped comfort Kim for 30 minutes until the paramedics could evacuate her. Heroes are people like Officer Randy Hernandez who held my hand while we were trapped in the car and prayed for Kim and me.

Heroes are the paramedics, doctors and nurses who perform their profession with such incredible competence and compassion. Heroes are life rescue helicopter pilots who are, sadly, constantly busy.

Heroes are people who run, operate, staff, and support places like Yaffe House, where families of patients can find some renewal and relief from the stark realities of the hospital.

Heroes are people like our parents – Kim's and mine – who are so selflessly taking care of what is most important to Kim and me – Olivia – during a time when we cannot, instead of being absorbed with their own worry and grief.

My cousin Barry and his wife Rene are heroes for their generous love and support for all of us. They just got married, are starting a new business and have a ton on their plates. Seems like all they have been doing is running around helping us, bringing me milkshakes and being generous beyond belief.

My sister Margot is a hero. Moments after the accident, she made sure that Olivia was safe and away from the car when she realized that Kim or I couldn't do so. She comforted Olivia and made sure she was thoroughly evaluated and never left her side.

Heroes are people who honor God in their service to others.

And, of course, Kim is a hero. She has courage, toughness, determination, good humor, incredible faith, and, of course, brutal honesty about her situation. If we did not have our faith, friends, families (and Olivia, of course), and the foundation of love for each other, it would be emotionally crippling to face the realities of what has happened. But we are blessed that we can look at these things with both honesty and optimism because, fortunately, that foundation of love and faith seems to be strong. It will surely be tested.

Kim is also my hero because she allows me to be free from the barriers I often erect to protect myself, and her, from the pain that too easily waits outside. I am very good at "faking it" and I often rely on it just to get by. I cannot get away with that with her, nor should I.

In the brief quiet moments that I got to spend yesterday with my hero, we were able to hug each other, pray together, cry a little, and rejoice a little. My hero allows me, like no one else, to be bold and also to be scared. As I grow further each day into manhood and fatherhood, I am blessed to have my hero holding my hand as we together navigate some uncharted waters.

TV and pop culture can take Barry Bonds, or Michael, or Peyton, or Tiger or any star athlete-of-the-moment as its hero. In the game of life, however, I have all the heroes I need...and I'm married to the biggest of them all.

Much sooner than I wanted, I had to direct my attention to some of the issues that had continued to go on even while we were having our little crisis. I knew that "life went on," but I dearly wished that it could have paused itself, even for a brief moment, after we had been ejected. The game of life would have demonstrated good sportsmanship if it had allowed us to catch our breath. Instead, we were afforded neither an injury time-out nor a standing eight-count. Consequently, I had to stick my head back into the real world and deal with things that needed my attention, though certainly not my enthusiasm.

The next morning – after I rinsed off the residue from my immersion back into the real world – your mother called me from her hospital room, which was remarkable in itself: I could hear her clearly. Her positive transition from tubes to mouthing words to whispering to really audible speech was astounding. On this day, your mother had one clear, supreme objective: she said, "I want to spend as much time with Olivia as possible." All I could say was, "Hallelujah!" That was the best medicine possible for both of you. For me, too.

We always tried to end our days with high notes and on high spirits. On this particular day, which was already great, your mother invited all of us to her room so that we could watch the Charlie Brown "Great Pumpkin" Halloween special on her hospital TV.

Things may have been simpler in Charlie Brown's time, but Charles Schultz's gift was realizing that the melancholy we all experience from those losing moments in life should always tempered with and surrounded by love. Charlie Brown always got another chance to kick (and miss) the football because he was loved. We, too, must always be grateful to know just how blessed and loved we are. And that is what keeps us going.

I need to remind myself of that constantly. Especially at night, when my mind-chatter often breaks through the silence of idle moments and too easily conspires to create horrifying thoughts of all that might have been.

CHAPTER SIX

DISCONNECTED

Crises don't happen on schedule.

BAD THINGS CAN HAPPEN TO GOOD PEOPLE in great places and during joyous occasions. Although we sometimes imagined that something bad could happen, we rationalized such thinking with the assumption that it probably wouldn't involve us, and at the very least, it certainly wouldn't be today. It was easy to postpone the thought of preparation. Preparing for a sudden adverse event is far different from contemplating, preparing, and planning for old age and retirement. There are some things for which one can never adequately prepare.

Of course, bad things happen to everyone, eventually. We just got ours earlier than most.

At some point during our stay in Denver, I began to comprehend the devastation ravaged on us by the Dragon. We were still in total "survival mode," needing to attend to the most immediate concerns and, at the most basic level, keep it together. The crisis management theories I knew from business were wholly inadequate for dealing with our situation. To keep myself from going crazy, I established only two objectives for my family and me. They were:

1) Get out of this *alive;* and

2) Get out of this *together.*

The problem is that I did not have the practical wherewithal or knowledge about how to achieve those goals. I was no Superman, and although I always pretended to be Batman, my virtual utility belt contained inappropriate tools. Only in a moment of quiet anguish did I realize that the only things that could pull us through were faith, hope, and love. Some people in my world considered such things to be mere concepts, beliefs, or ideals that were contrived attempts to make ourselves feel better. I considered them to be universal truths because they pointed to the source of their origin: a higher power of creation and unfathomable love.

The Dragon had left its visible imprint on your mother. Her body had been physically disconnected from itself in a way that was tragically debilitating. The Dragon's breath inside me, however, was less visible. It was subtle and, thus, insidious. I began to see that it was trying to do whatever it could to separate me from that which I held dear. That is, anything that I associated with faith, hope, and love.

Not long after the accident, I received a bundle of mail from some friends back in San Francisco who were taking care of our dogs, Duffy and Sparky. The giant envelope had the faint but distinctive smell of the Dragon's breath. I took a deep breath and stiffened my back. The envelope contained more than the usual fluffy junk mail. But then an enormous stack of bills and statements cascaded out of the envelope. How could so much paper be generated by the medical and insurance industries in such short order? We had been gone only about ten days, and much of this mail had made a circuitous route to us in Denver by way of San Francisco.

The ungainly mound that catapulted into the otherwise protective confines caused my stomach to churn yet again. This load of mail was yet another assault, and its invasion penetrated far beyond my normal lines of defense. Its effect was immediate and piercing: As I tore into the mail, I was also tearing off the covers of all the fatigue, frustration, and resentful anguish that had been silently accumulating since the accident. Like my buried emotions, this was the kind of mail that was unwelcome and that I didn't want to confront and deal with. However, because "life goes on," I realized that these problems wouldn't go away; if unaddressed, they would grow and create more serious issues down the road. Just like my emotions.

The first letter I tore into was from our utility provider, informing me of its intent to turn off our gas and electric service in San Francisco because we were a week past due with our bill. After tearing into this letter, I wanted to tear into *them*. I had not missed a monthly payment to this company in ten years. They were, of course, kind enough to send a separate 48-hour notice (which I also hadn't seen), although they hadn't thought of calling first to explore the situation.

Unfortunately, my experience with PG&E was only a taste of what was lying ahead. It was my first real foreshadowing of "the System," which was invoked, if not created, by the Dragon. "The System" soon became a primary weapon in the Dragon's arsenal to further wreak havoc in our lives.

Several hours later, done for the day, I put aside my paperwork and took another dose of my narcotic cocktail. I asked myself if those things were addictive. I knew the answer to that, of course: only if you let them. My reasoning was lame and I knew it. I surely needed the drugs, but I could sense the Tormentor inside give me a little dig, as it burrowed a little deeper, settling into its now-comfortable new home.

One of the things I quickly learned when we were in "survival mode" was that I quickly became very preoccupied with all kinds of things I never before knew existed. I learned new things about injuries, hospitals, medicine, insurance, and, of course, paper. I also learned a lot about others and about myself. I had to make many decisions about things I had never before considered. It became a very busy time, and because I had never been there before, everything had a sense of urgency about it that kept my adrenaline working overtime. Truthfully, I found strange comfort in simple engagement – in a constant state of active "busy-ness." Staying active served as a handy distraction and effective tactic to avoid confronting directly the situation at hand. It also made me feel like I was doing something useful and helping out. The danger was that such "busy-ness" was conveniently disguised to circumvent the real need to more fully connect and play a meaningfully integral part of the situation. The busier I was, the more disconnected I became.

I then thought about your mother, how her body had been broken, and how she was probably disconnected from it in every way. She had also lost the sensation of feeling God's presence in our lives. Perhaps I was too preoccupied to notice because I was trying to keep us and everything together. I remember your mother asking me, "Why isn't God here with us now, when we need Him most? Why can't we feel Him?"

The clear answer to her troubling question was that we were too busy. That sense of hectic activity, at least for me, overpowered my desire to be with God first. We indeed needed to re-establish our connection to God, but we didn't know how to do so because our bodies, our minds, and our spirits had been disconnected. No one said to us, "I'll carry the message to God for you," because no one knew that was what we really needed, and we didn't really know how to tell anyone.

I knew that people were doing their best to help us through prayer and support, but we really needed someone to tell us, point blank: 'This is a time when you have to let the rest of us carry you.'

That would have eased my mind so much, just knowing for certain that our connection to God was not completely severed.

Of course, God *was* always with us. We just didn't always realize it. Which was exactly the Dragon's intention.

CRISES DON'T HAPPEN ON SCHEDULE

In the world of my time, few people expected to be in a crisis or severe adverse event. Nevertheless, crises of all varieties did indeed happen all the time. If you suddenly find yourself part of some adverse event, I offer the following thoughts and suggestions. They are based solely on my own experiences. Some of these suggestions are ones I used; others are ones I wish I had.

In hindsight, if I had been smart, I would have admitted the magnitude of my confusion and sought help from sources that might have had previous experience with such injuries, accidents, and logistics of the aftermath. I should have made a blanket plea for help to hospital, police, fire, and EMS staff, confessing my ignorance and asking for a road map of what we would need to do to start reconstructing our lives. The truth is that my ignorant pride prevented me from even admitting that I had no clue. I thought I could figure it out as we went along. Such logic, very sound while in the moment (under duress, drugs, and delusion), seemed noble and courageous at the time. After the fact, however, it was an enormous waste of time, energy, and potential resources that could have prevented much of the anguish, uncertainty, and wheel-spinning I subsequently encountered.

Unfortunately, I later realized that no such map really existed. Many of these agencies and resources dealt with very discrete issues and then handed off the situation to someone else. In a broader sense, no one really knew what to do or whom to turn to for better answers or solutions. A blanket question like, "What do we do next?" drew a painful silence. For what it's worth, here are some of my suggestions, should you find yourself in situation like I was in, where I didn't know what I didn't know.

1. SEEK ASSISTANCE

EMOTIONAL AND SPIRITUAL

Seek out and connect with a trusted person who can be your confidential spiritual and emotional guide. If no one comes to mind, have a close friend find someone for you. You will need to lean hard on this person, so make sure he or she has the ability and *availability* to carry you when you need it. Ideally, you want someone who knows when to listen and when to offer counsel, as you will need both. You may need more than one person, but you will need someone, preferably not your spouse and probably someone not related. You don't want either of you feeling awkward.

MEDICAL

Through a trusted friend, associate, or professional, assign a case manager to whom all other medical specialists report. This person should have an overall perspective of the primary medical goals and a firm understanding of how they can be achieved. This person should represent the patient and/or caregiver in helping to make medical decisions that best serve the primary objectives. Each specialist often works as if in a silo, partitioned off from others. The medical case manager interacts with all of them, thereby helping to coordinate the best possible outcome.

LEGAL

Assign a power of attorney to a trusted friend or relative. A power of attorney or proof of legal guardianship is required to discuss, for example, even the silliest, most basic issue with a medical or insurance representative. Sadly, it's the law (designed to protect our rights to privacy), but it can make for very long, frustrating encounters. Outsource as much of possible to someone else.

INSURANCE

Talk to a financial planner early in life. Buy more insurance than you think you'll need, or at least more than you currently need. Getting insurance after an adverse life event is both expensive and pointless. If you're not partially prepared for an initial crisis, it is almost impossible to get prepared for a subsequent one. As much as possible, be ready so you don't have to get ready while in the midst of the chaos of a crisis.

2. CONNECT WITH YOUR EXISTING NETWORKS

Connect with one responsible member from each group and put that person in charge of that particular group. Then connect the leaders with each other. Appoint one as "chair" in order to coordinate tasks and communications on your behalf. You want to delegate as much as possible without having to repeat the orders multiple times. If you cannot connect personally with a person from each of these groups, then select someone to serve as your representative to do it for you.

Tell them what has transpired. Make sure the selected point person from each group sets up a user group or distribution list within his or her organization for efficient communications. Tell them of your needs or of your questions, concerns, and frustrations. Ask for help if you know what you need. Solicit suggestions if you do not. Create a list of tasks and chores that others can do for you.

3. SEEK AND ASK FOR FORGIVENESS

Don't blame yourself for your current situation, but seek forgiveness for past transgressions, including ones you don't even know about. You will also need to extend forgiveness to anyone for whom you hold a grudge. It is nearly impossible to ask for help when your heart carries the burdens of unresolved umbrage or some hidden guilt from resentment that others harbor against you.

You, my dear child, have convinced me that all of us, as babies, are actually little angels that transform ourselves into human form once we decide to land in our parents' arms. Babies are special because, among other things, they see things that we as adults no longer can. As it is, the world soon intrudes on our domain and quickly succeeds in separating us from our original, angelic form. We have a choice how far we want to be separated from our original form. Our decisions and actions determine our disconnectedness.

I believe that this is the true origin of Murphy's Law. We start out perfect in God's likeness, and then the Dragon conspires to mess us up. Eventually, we desperately realize that our primary goal in life is to get back to the state in which we started.

People experience many different kinds of crises, each of which is unique to those who endure them. But they are the same in that each is intended to bring us to our knees. Ultimately, the only way to conquer the crisis is to first succumb to it. We have to bring our hands together in submission…but look up, not down.

CHAPTER SEVEN

First Move

One form of hell is to be stir-crazy…when you can barely stir.

*I*T WAS TIME TO GET OUT OF DENVER. It was time to act and do something, even if it was as insignificant as your mother and me trying to wiggle our big toes. Or *deciding* to try and wiggle our big toes. Action often starts with a conscious decision to do something, as opposed to *not* doing something (which, of course, is also a conscious decision).

Nevertheless, even *deciding* to try and move our toes was significant because we had no idea if we'd be able to move them. Your mother could not move any part of her body below her chest, and my foot had been crushed. Nevertheless, the simple act of deciding to try to move was itself noteworthy because it engaged our minds to visualize moving from a state of inertia into a state of motion. That's why the first move is always mental. The mind prepares the way for the body to follow. That initial, important thrust may not always be seen, but it can always be felt.

Basic, natural movement doesn't require much thought when a body works well. Years of post-infanthood practice render routine most simple body movements. Even with more complex, athletic

movements, enough practice removes a lot of the mental preparation to engage in the mechanics. The truth is that practice does not
make perfect; practice makes *progress*.

However, if a body doesn't work well or has been compromised,
those once-automatic body movements require a lot more physical
and *conscious* effort. And, because a mind can be a terrible thing, fear
of failure creeps into the picture and tries to claim a leading role. Fear
was one of those things the Dragon left behind. The Dragon's breath
was fear. Fear of failure made the first move – the mental one, the one
that mattered most – highly risky because we exposed ourselves to
possible defeat. How would we respond if we couldn't move our toes?
Would we loathe ourselves and sink into despair? Then what would
we do? Where would we go? It required courage.

I began to question whether courage could truly exist without
faith. I am not referring to bravery, which I think of as an isolated,
definable event that might involve pain or discomfort. Like getting
a tooth pulled, eating yogurt well beyond its expiration date, or vol-
unteering to be the goaltender on your local dart team.

Bravery to me implied an attitude of toughness and taking a
stiff upper lip regarding potential consequences. Such bravery was
good, but it was different from courage, which implied a greater
awareness of the consequences, ones that were willingly endured, if
necessary. More importantly, courage implied that I was *not* really
all that brave but that I would persevere in spite of my weaknesses
or fears, of which I was fully aware.

To me, bravery involved denying my fear, or at least overcoming
it by drawing on my inner strength and determination. Courage, on
the other hand, involved acknowledging my fear and then overcoming it by drawing on an external strength to carry on regardless. In
my case, external strength came from faith. It was my complete and
utter conviction that God is good. If I trusted that I would ultimately

end up with Him, I could endure or tolerate anything that might happen to me.

STUCK IN A MOMENT...HIT THE BUTTON

Late one night, while still in the SICU (Surgical Intensive Care Unit), your mother started experiencing severe discomfort. We had placed a radio and CD player by her bedside to provide some soothing sounds and a buffer from the buzz of the machines around her and the constant chaos on her ward of the severely injured. Usually, the music helped to distract her from the disconcerting noises that invaded any reasonable expectation of sleep or rest. On this particular night, however, the irritant was the CD player itself: a CD had gotten "stuck" and was skipping, playing the same three-second track over and over.

Normally, such a situation was remedied quite easily. The nurse staff always placed a "call button" device in your mother's right hand so that she could solicit assistance by simply pressing the button with her thumb. She had regained enough strength and motor skills in her right hand that this was not a problem, although it was still very challenging with her left hand.

The call button provided a comforting sense of assurance to anyone being held captive in a hospital bed. The most critical element of the call button, however, was its proximity to the patient who may have needed to use it. It was better to be a lost wanderer crawling through a vast desert in a desperate search for water than a suffering patient trying to ring a hospital call button that was agonizingly beyond her reach.

The stuck CD was driving your mother crazy, and the CD player was well beyond her reach, perched on a table far from her hospital bed. Your mother had to choose between either going the entire night with the skipping CD or trying to reach her call button. The challenge, of course, was locating the darned call button.

At this moment, your mother began to realize the extent of her injury. When she tried to move her head to look for the button, her head didn't respond by turning the direction she willed it, and it didn't help that she was wearing a big, cumbersome neck brace. Nevertheless, her head was just stuck…much like the CD that was driving her crazy.

So, your mother extended her eyes peripherally, as if trying to see something behind her ears, while having to keep her head stationary. At last, she located the call button. It was dangling off the side railing of her bed, quite close to her right hand but not within easy reach for someone recently paralyzed. Technically, she wasn't supposed to be able to move her arms. Decision time: accept the condition or try to do something about it.

The CD was driving her nuts. Not being able to reach the call button was driving her *more* nuts. She embarked on a quest that would test the depths of her determination and set the stage for all her subsequent progress. She decided to reach for the call button. It took all of her strength and concentration. It took all her courage. And it took her to a place of realizing just how badly injured she was, and to making a decision that she was not going to be a helpless victim, if she had a choice in the matter.

For the next two hours, your mother struggled to reach that call button. Though it rested only inches from her right hand (thankfully, the hand capable of even attempting any such movement), the call button must have appeared miles away. It was like climbing the final and most difficult stretch of a mountain summit: the last few steps require the most effort and energy. If she made it, she achieved glory. If she failed, she might have died – not physically, but she would have been buried emotionally.

Obviously, she made it. I would not have carried on like this if she hadn't. It is a telling anecdote, however, because it set the foundation for a determined and committed approach to rehabilitation that enabled your mother to claim victory over an obstacle that was completely beyond anyone's realm of expectation. As a result, such victories became for her almost commonplace.

When your mother was finally able to "hit the button," it was like hitting the after-burners on a fighter jet. She propelled herself into a different stratosphere. In the span of two hours, your mother went from comprehending fully the magnitude of her injury to deciding to take as much control as possible over her eventual recovery. Instead of being trapped and stuck in a moment, she decided to hit the button and change the outcome.

We cannot control what happens to us, but we can control how we respond.

LEAVING DENVER

We were eager to leave Denver, and so was our health insurance company, which did not have a contract with St. Anthony Hospital. Through the magic of accounting, our insurer discovered that it was far less expensive – and thus more desirable – to fly your mother and me on a special medical Lear jet than to stay a few more days at St. Anthony. So away we went.

We were shipped off by ambulance to meet the jet at a private airstrip not far from Bronco Stadium. A light snow started falling as we pulled into the jet hanger. Inside was only one plane, which I assumed was ours. *Wow,* I thought, *this thing is tiny!* The crew introduced themselves to us. There was a pilot, a co-pilot, and two nurses. They made brief introductions and then the pilot encouraged us to hustle, given the worsening weather. Your mother was on a stretcher and connected to a ventilator as well as some bags of medication and hydration fluid. I was hobbling around on crutches and moving well, all things considered.

The most important objective of the flight was to ensure that your mother was kept stable. Excess turbulence would hurt her fragile neck and spine, and sudden changes in air pressure would have very dangerous effects on her respiratory system, which had also been severely compromised in the accident.

I heard the crew discussing amongst themselves your mother's various injuries and hoping that she was strong enough to endure the flight. One of the nurses finally looked at your mother and must have seen her determination and fighting spirit. She turned to the others and said, "It's a short flight. She'll be fine."

The pilot of the plane then looked at me quizzically and asked, "Are you coming too?"

"You bet," I responded enthusiastically. "Why?"

"Well…" He hesitated, "we weren't really expecting you."

"And he's tall," chimed in one of the other crewmembers.

"I'm not *that* tall," I countered. "What's wrong with being tall?"

"Nothing, really," answered the pilot, "except that the plane is quite…small."

"Yeah," I said, "I can see that. How do you get in there?" I asked, looking inside the open door. I saw many instruments and machines, but no creature comforts. No snack cart offering beverage service or hot towels.

"I think we can take you," asserted the pilot, "but you'll have to squeeze way in the back."

"Sure, I can do that," I said, agreeably, "but 'way' back isn't very far. It's like, maybe, two feet. This is plane is *small*." I thought Lear jets were supposed to be roomy and luxurious.

"No, keep going," he said encouragingly, as I shimmied through the door and snaked my way through the tiny fuselage. "Keep going.

You'll have to sit on those canvas bags and jackets behind that seat. Yes, that's it...*way* back there."

The crew then began to move your mother on board. This took some careful maneuvering, but these guys had obviously done this before. They made it look easy. Your mother was kept on her stretcher, which was tightly secured by belts and other stabilizers. She stayed in her position, lying on her back.

I still can't believe we all fit in that tiny tin can, but I loved every minute of it. We were heading into a whole new world, but at least we would all be together. Unfortunately, we didn't really know where that world would be, which implied that any road would take us there. In our case, we had to build our own road. We had no tools, only desire and determination. To get started, we had to shuffle our feet. Or, in our case, decide to wiggle our big toes.

CHAPTER EIGHT

LA TESTAROSSA

Without faith, vision is impossible.

YOUR MOTHER – AND MOST WOMEN IN MY TIME – thought that most men were nuts in our fascination with exotic cars. Women failed to understand our appreciation for the sophisticated artistic symbolism that represented each man's quest for love. Cars represented our reverence for women and our literal pursuit of them. We appreciated these cars for their expressed beauty and their obvious power.

For most people in my world, the moniker that first came to mind and most easily (and longingly) rolled off the tongue was *Ferrari*. Among Ferrari's boldest creations, the *Testarossa* stood out as a supreme combination of striking beauty, unapologetically over-abundant power, and a sophisticated, yet unpretentiously gracious posture. The *Testarossa* inspired wonder, admiration and respect that few other cars could match.

We could not help but take notice of a *Testarossa*, whether we saw it, heard it, or felt it. Everything about it implied that it was unique and special. Among all manufactured creations that combined design and function, the *Testarossa* was, perhaps, the ultimate timeless expression of art and machine. The only logical color for a *Testarossa* was red – Ferrari simply *implied* red, and more simply, the English translation of *Testarossa* is "red head."

Your mother had brilliant red hair. She also had the beauty, fire, passion, and engine of a *Testarossa*. Her engine, of course, was her spirit, compassion, and a strong-willed sense of independence. Most women of any era probably would not want to be compared to a sports car, but the *Testarossa* was no ordinary sports car. And your mother was no ordinary woman.

These qualities in your mother arose out of the harsh, stark environment where she grew up: Odessa, in the West Texas oil patch. The part of West Texas where your mother was raised was hot, flat, dry, and dusty. At that time, Odessa was to natural beauty what deep-fried Spam was to good nutrition. If Odessa were a blank canvas, it's conceivable that even Leonardo or Michelangelo would have walked away, despairingly uninspired.

Odessa was a tough, rugged place. It was hot. But it was oil country, which was the only reason why people would live there. The Permian Basin, on which Odessa lay, contained enormous oil and natural gas deposits. The oil and gas business could be extremely lucrative, but it was not for the faint of heart. The people that industry attracted had to be tough, resilient, and resourceful.

To illustrate the creativity of kids raised in such a boringly hostile – and hot – environment, your mother told me of the numerous times that she and her friends dug holes in the ground and covered them with chicken wire and old blankets as a means to escape the heat of summer. I asked her if any of her friends had tree forts that they could climb into. "Tree forts?" she responded, incredulously. "We didn't even know what tree forts were. We didn't even have trees!" Did I mention that Odessa was barren?

Odessa made up for its lack of trees and tree forts with a forest of oil and gas rigs. It was an eerie sight. You would probably look at these gangly steel structures and think that they were giant, man-made mosquitoes designed to suck oil out from under the earth's skin. You wouldn't be far off in your thinking. Oil, in fact, had become our world's life-blood.

The oil business was highly volatile. Accordingly, West Texas was notorious for exaggerated booms and busts, which resulted in the prevailing fortunes and misfortunes of assorted wildcatters and mosquito-vampire operators. The one constant source of entertainment, pride, and community connection was (and still is, I believe) the high school football team.

H.G. Bissinger wonderfully portrayed this in his book *Friday Night Lights*. Your grandparents and many resident Odessans hated the book because they felt betrayed by Bissinger after they had graciously allowed him into their community. As an East Coast Yankee, I found the book to be endearing in its depiction of a community that came together in support of its team and, ultimately, each other. There seemed to be a real sense of upholding the small-town values that had long since vanished from the American landscape we romanticized. Sure, the football games themselves were important, but it was not really about the game: it was about them, as a community, just being together and supporting each other as best they could.

Thus was hatched your mother's addiction to Texas football. I used to assume, as a newly indoctrinated Texas football fan, that the pinnacle of football in Texas was achieved in college. The truth is that nothing compared with Texas high school football. If BBQ was the state food of Texas, then high school football was the state's religion.

Your mother recounted to me how several former players from her championship high school team, the Permian Panthers, found that playing at the college level was a real disappointment compared to the exhilarating passion and intensity of high school games. Some kids evidently quit their college programs or even dropped out of school entirely, feeling that their experiences from high school could be never surpassed. But such was the danger of many small towns, where people tried to re-live the dream – long after it had passed – and never allowed themselves to envision a new one.

As I became better acquainted with Odessa, I began to get a clearer understanding of your mother: her frenzy for football, her eyes that thirsted for natural beauty, and her quest for greener pastures in which to plant herself and create a life in fertile soil.

Your mother was smart and excelled in school, so gaining admission to the University of Texas in Austin was not a big deal. She was part of a family legacy that included five generations of alumni. I presume the first words she spoke as a baby were, "Hook 'em Horns!" Austin was also a nirvana-like reprieve from the oppressive conditions of Odessa. Your mother had developed asthma as a child, not severe, but bad enough so that Odessa's climate often forced her to turn to her inhaler. She always carried one with her.

In addition, after your mother graduated from high school, a small tumor was detected on her left lung. It required surgery that resulted in part of her lung being removed. This left her even more ill equipped to breathe in a harsh environment. But the tumor strengthened further her already-solid faith. The pioneering spirit found in places like Odessa also required faith in God to persevere and be sustained during times of challenge and hardship.

Your mother attended Young Life as a teenager. Young Life was a Christian organization that helped prepare adolescents for the future, and it helped create in her a foundation of faith that I could discern the first time I met her. I admired it and wished I had built a similar foundation when I was younger. Your mother's strong faith was one of the key things that drew me to her.

Our mutual faith helped keep us together. When my faith faltered, your mother was there to back me up and lift me up. I may have been more vocal and outwardly spiritual, but your mother had a far deeper relationship with God than I did. She would never tell you, but I can.

Soon after surviving the lung surgery, your mother shipped off to college in Austin. Back in the days when I was scared of anything Texan, Austin stood out as a place to avoid at all costs. My imagination ran wild. People there are weird, I thought. They are also Liberal as hell, and they don't wear shoes; they wear Birkenstocks. My paranoia, you can see, grasped at anything to justify itself.

Your mother, knowing of my fear, kindly and patiently introduced me to aspects of Austin to help me overcome my Yankee stereotypes. Before taking me on a trip there, she wisely educated me on little factoids that I found to be rather interesting, if not downright impressive. For example:

- There were more PhDs per capita in Austin than any other U.S. city.
- UT Austin was the largest public university in the country.
- UT had the largest endowment of any public university in the country.
- There were more Blues clubs in a four-block radius in Austin than the combined music clubs of most other cities.
- The state capitol in Austin was larger than any other in the U.S., and the only state capitol allowed by law to be taller than the U.S. Capitol in Washington, D.C.
- There were lots and lots of bats in Austin, and they consumed about 20,000 tons of mosquitoes…every night.

At long last, I tightened my belt and agreed to travel with your mother to Texas. I couldn't completely suppress my Yankee-born prejudices, so I had to tease your mother about how many trucks with gun racks we would see. I goaded her like this for weeks prior to our trip. "I really want to see some honest Texans," I would say. "You know, the kind with horns on the front of their pickups and loaded guns on the back."

"Don't be silly," she would counter, "people in Austin don't have guns." I drove her crazy with the gun jokes.

When we finally landed in Austin, we emerged from the airport and stood outside waiting for your grandparents to pick us up. Lo and behold, the *very first* vehicle that drove by us was a pickup truck…majestically adorned with a spectacular set of long horns on the hood and a full gun rack on the back window. I jumped up and down and rolled on the ground, laughing harder than I ever had in my life. Your mother's parents then drove up and thought that I'd lost my mind. Your mother wanted to ship me back home.

In spite of that (or probably because of it), I fell in love with Austin, as well as all the other parts of Texas I came to know. I cannot tell whether I loved Texas because of Texas or because of your mother. Regardless, it was she who introduced me to Texas, so she gets the credit. And the blame.

Your mother also introduced me to Italy. Do you sense a theme here? Your mother introduced me to most of the good things in my life, especially herself. Similar to my youthful fear of Texas, I viewed Italy with considerable trepidation, if not disdain. My mother was born in Germany, and so I was raised with a high regard for Northern European sensibilities. Those *Southern* Europeans (and especially those *Italians*) were so…*chaotic*. What I didn't realize then, of course, was that their chaos was simply a more flamboyant expression of…*passion*. I finally started to get it. Thanks to your mother, Italy became my favorite place on the planet. We had dreamed of some-day living there, in the tiny coastal village of Positano.

Among the other great things that your mother introduced to me was the profound notion that believing came before visual con-firmation. In other words, whereas common wisdom (the greatest of all oxymorons) dictated that we had to first see something in order to believe it, your mother made me aware of the fundamental tru-ism underlying any decent faith. That is: *believe* first, and then we will see. That subtle mind-shift completely altered my outlook on life and, as you will see, helped create for our family a reconnecting bridge that otherwise would have never been attempted or contem-plated. Without some sort of faith, vision was impossible.

Another gift your mother gave me was an open acceptance of offbeat, wacky humor, and we shared a love of things that were odd or slightly off-color. More importantly, she helped me reconcile the inner conflict I wrestled with that such appreciation was diametri-cally opposite to the Christian doctrine I so dearly needed for my salvation. In other words, your mother helped ease the burden I had put on myself, the one where everything needed to be righteous but, also, very *heavy*. She emphasized this by pointing out that God must have an outrageous sense of humor because He created dogs. A quick glance at a pedigree chart confirmed that there were indeed some funny-looking pooches out there. I think God must have taken delight both in His creations and in our finding pleasure and good-natured humor in them.

Not coincidentally, only your mother could help me fully appre-ciate, after much contemplation, one of the greatest lines in English literature, penned by the incomparable Hunter S. Thompson:

"When the going gets tough, the weird turn pro." (Fear and Loathing in Las Vegas)

I found that line to be more relevant with each passing year. It became yet another reminder that being easily amused was a great asset in managing with the ups, the downs, and the great unknowns. It also enabled me to realize that I was always capable of having a far more expansive and creative perspective. The same holds true for you, whether you currently believe in God or just do not yet realize that you do.

You're packing a suitcase for a place
None of us has been.
A place that has to be believed
Before it is seen.
(U2 – "Walk On")

Your mother began her career as a nurse. She had a passion for helping people that was fueled by both her Christian faith and her close call with cancer when she was graduating from high school. Your mother wanted to give back because she felt blessed to be given a second chance. The great training ground for young medical professionals was in the emergency rooms (ERs) of major hospitals. Many of your mother's nurse friends gravitated to the ERs because of the training and the excitement. Your mother didn't seek the excitement; she'd had plenty of her own from personal experience. Instead, she chose to work in the Cancer Care Unit (CCU), the place for patients who were so sick that survival was hoped for but not generally expected.

Your mother comforted these very sick patients in their last, dying days. She ministered to them in the middle of the night. When they died, she would pray for them, and she would stay with them until the bodies were taken away. She thought it wasn't right for people to die alone.

During the early and mid-1980s, the patient composition of the Cancer Care Unit changed dramatically. It went from predominantly cancer patients to almost exclusively AIDS patients. It was as if an inferno had consumed a giant apartment building with thousands of tenants, all of whom arrived in the CCU in never-ending waves. They kept coming, and dying. Another wave would come…and everyone would die. It was like a giant conveyor belt of death. Body bags were flying everywhere, just to keep up. It became too much.

Your mother left the hospital to join a biotechnology company, where she was put in charge of clinical trials for novel cancer treatments. She did well and was eventually recruited to run the Oncology Research Program for a consortium of Bay Area hospitals. She knew medicine, she knew healthcare, and she knew good practice.

All of these skills would prove invaluable in helping her deal with her own injuries. Your mother's training, for example, helped her catch so many potential problems and faulty procedures such that, without her own intervention, she would have likely had serious setbacks or complications.

Shortly after the accident, I recall wishing that I – and not your mother – had been the one paralyzed and put in a wheelchair. I thought to myself (rather stoically, if not heroically) that I was better equipped to meet the challenges of paralysis because I was stronger and tougher. I would have gladly changed places with your mother if I could have.

But the truth is that your mother was far better equipped than me. Sure, she understood medicine and issues surrounding the body; but that is knowledge she would have imparted on my behalf as well. The real difference is that she was far stronger and tougher than I ever could have been. She had inner strength and determination that were positive motivators. More important, she had a peace and grace that could withstand the greatest challenges and torment. Had I been in her place, I am certain that I would have become an ogre. I would have cast anger and misery throughout our house.

Your mother, on the other hand, grew more resolved that she would not be defined by her physical condition. It never detracted from her character. In fact, she used it as an opportunity to be more loving, compassionate and merciful.

CHAPTER NINE

PIERCING THE VEIL

Our worlds are oceans apart,
yet separated by a thin veil right in front of you.

OUR MEDICAL LEAR JET TOUCHED DOWN in San Jose. The weather was warm and welcoming, compared to the chill and snow of Denver. Local paramedics greeted us, and they drove us from the airport to the hospital. Unfortunately, they had a hard time finding out exactly where in the hospital to deliver us.

Our little entourage was completely lost, and we challenged every corridor to be the one that would lead us to our assigned destination. This was a big hospital, and no one knew who we were, where we were, or what we were doing there. The paramedics tried calling everyone under the sun, pleading for direction: "Where the heck are we? Where are we supposed to go? How are we supposed to get there?" I had been asking myself those same questions since the accident.

FREQUENCY

After wandering the hospital halls like nomads for what seemed like years, we finally found the unit where your mother was supposed to go. The protective bubble of Denver exploded in our faces when we entered our new reality in San Jose. As we were about to enter the hospital's Rehabilitation Unit, a word kept popping into my mind: "Frequency." I knew that hospitals had a different pace and rhythm and that I would have to re-calibrate my frequency to be more compatible with the hospitals. As the word repeated itself in my head, its rhythm began to play around on the various syllables. Suddenly, the word "frequency" began to play itself in my head as a warning siren, *"Free-Quen-Cy...Freeq-Uen-Cy...Freeq-Uen-Cee."* Then it hit me: *"Freak-When-See"* as in, "you're going to Freak When you See it." Which was indeed the case, profoundly and frequently.

Your mother's new home was at Santa Clara Valley Medical Center. It was a hospital that was nicknamed, appropriately, "Valley." In my time and in that part of the world, "the Valley" meant only one thing: Silicon Valley. The cruel logic of the hospital's nickname didn't hit me until later, when I started recalling my vivid associations of "Valley," none of which were exactly uplifting images of life and recovery.

A hospital's name had considerable influence on how its patients perceived the quality of care and thus, their relative prospects. It helped for a hospital to have a name that sounded encouraging, inspirational, and uplifting, or one that simply implied that a patient might be in good hands. For example, a name such as "Shady Hill Hospital" sounded nicely calming, restful, and therapeutic, the kind of place likely to promote recovery and rehabilitation. Similarly, any place named after a religious place or person at least suggested an obvious solicitation of a higher power to bestow healing powers on the facility, the staff, and the patients.

Unfortunately, the only images my mind associated with "Valley" were not positive. They were things like Death Valley, you know, like walking through the Valley of the Shadow of Death,

Valley of the Dead, Valley of Despair, Valley of Doom, Valley of Locusts, Valley of Darkness, Valley of Perpetual Suffering, Valley of Suffocating Smog, Valley of Weak Coffee. The last few were my own projections, but I think you get my drift.

Compared to the almost gentile conditions at St. Anthony in Denver, the atmosphere and aura at Valley completely shocked us. St. Anthony, sponsored by the Catholic Church, felt safe and nurturing. It was clean, and seemed acutely aware that a patient's sense of dignity could be influenced by the atmosphere and surroundings.

In contrast, Valley seemed like a makeshift Army hospital set up on the outskirts of Baghdad. Compared to the fastidiously spotless conditions we had in Denver, Valley seemed filthy. We assumed it was antiseptically clean because the place reeked of ammonia and other cleansers designed to wipe out evil little germs. Much like an over-cologned person who hasn't bathed in days, the smell at Valley only heightened our concern about what it was covering up.

Your mother started to cry. She wanted to turn around and return to Denver, and I didn't blame her; I had learned to like it there, or at least I liked the idea of going back to our protective little bubble.

The conditions at Valley were not, I would come to appreciate, the result or fault of the dedicated and conscientious Valley staff but, rather, were another by-product of the injustices perpetuated by the System. St. Anthony was a private hospital; Valley was public and was owned by a county. This created a big difference in who got paid how much and for what.

Reluctantly, we tried it, as we really had little alternative. It may not have looked pretty, but the quality of care, we were assured, was excellent. It turned out that Valley was one of 17 so-called "Centers of Excellence" in the United States for Spinal Cord Injury (SCI) rehabilitation. The care did indeed turn out to be far better than the appearance of the facilities.

As we entered your mother's new home in the SCI unit, I assessed this strange new world. I sensed a level of pain and suffering more palpable and acute than any I had ever seen or experienced. It seemed like a war zone.

Many of the injuries were truly horrific. Everyone, like your mother, was paralyzed, which was bad enough. Others were paralyzed and needed to have limbs amputated. Others were paralyzed and could not speak. Others were also severely burned. A few also had brain injuries, which were especially insidious in their mysterious complexity. It was heart wrenching to see such suffering.

In this place were people trying to recover from catastrophic injuries that had altered their lives forever. The place was tragic and sad and terribly lonely. It was especially lonely for your mother and the other co-residents because they each felt like strangers in their own bodies. And it was lonely for me because I was unable to fully empathize with her. Nor could I comfort her in a way either of us understood. She was certainly paralyzed physically, but I was almost paralyzed emotionally.

We went deeper beyond the veil when we arrived at the SCI Rehabilitation Unit. Once we pierced the veil, we became part of a world that had once been invisible to us. Now that we were in that world, we would never be able to completely leave it.

After a couple of days, a social worker came to see if she could offer us government assistance. We weren't eligible for any, but I questioned her further.

"I understand your programs aren't appropriate for us," I continued, "but you must have seen many cases involving people like us. What would you recommend we do? We're very new at this."

"Well," she sighed, "the one course of action that a lot of people take is to file for divorce."

"Excuse me?!" I replied, not quite believing my ears.

"Oh yes," she went on, practically lighting up, as if buoyed by the prospect of entrusting us with a secret map that lead to a sacred treasure trove that only her beneficence allowed us to glimpse. "If a couple is divorced, then the disabled spouse is able to qualify for every available state and federal assistance program. It's really the only way to get decent assistance, especially when people are so disabled, so it's a very practical choice. In fact, it's really your most financially advantageous course of action."

I could not believe my ears. I was outraged at such a thought. The accident had taken your mother's legs, but I wasn't going to let it take our marriage as well.

When we pierced the veil, we soon learned that the divorce rate among married couples for which one partner had become disabled was something like 75%. That was a huge, sad number.

When we pierced the veil, we quickly realized how unprepared we were for our new reality. Whatever we had learned in all those years in school, and whatever skills we had developed in all those years in the workforce, were practically irrelevant in our new world. Furthermore, there was no handbook or road map.

When we pierced the veil, we very quickly started the natural process of looking around at our fellow citizens in our new world. By and large, everyone was checking each other out because we all wanted to make a connection. We also felt compelled to compare notes about how others wound up on this side of the veil. Everyone had a different story. All were incredibly tragic because, at the very least, every case affected more than just the life of the person injured or infirm.

An accident like ours, for example, touched many people, whether physically or emotionally. There was also a natural tendency for those who were injured to compare themselves relative to others in a similar condition. It was very easy for a person with an injury to look at a person with a less severe injury of the same variety and to think, "If only my injury were like his, instead of mine, then I'd be so much better off. Then I could handle this ordeal." Then, of course, all we had to do was look around the corner at the person whose injury was so much worse than ours. Then our hearts would break, and we would thank God that we were not as bad off as that person.

When we pierced the veil, we were able to discern between those who had some sort of faith and those who did not. Those differences were especially palpable in the Rehab Unit. We could make a distinction based on the quality of the air in different rooms.

Despite challenging circumstances, patients with faith had a measure of hope and optimism about the new journey ahead of them. Patients who did not were despondent and despairing. Those with faith looked forward. Those without faith looked back. Those with faith didn't seek to blame their situation on someone or something. Those without faith were often bitter and angry with a perceived perpetrator, the world, or themselves. Those with faith searched for new ways to live. Those without faith tried to reclaim the way they used to live. Those with faith tried to repel the Dragon. Those without faith didn't think it mattered.

When we pierced the veil, we did not take certain things for granted anymore. Silly things made a lot more sense and were more meaningful. Things once considered serious, became less significant. We started to see more of the injustices in our world, not because they affected us personally, but rather, because they ultimately affected everyone. When we pierced the veil, we realized that we were already in a place where most people were eventually going to travel, though they did not yet realize it.

NOV 11, 2002

WE NEVER RETURN HOME THE SAME

Yesterday, Kim moved her right foot...on command! Great news indeed. I truly believe that God is answering our prayers and working His miracles through Kim. While it is tempting to assume this great progress will be a leading indicator of future successes, we have to give thanks for all that we have right now, and not be too expectant of similar miracles.

Nevertheless, there are times when many people, even all the king's men, cannot prevent a fall from a precarious perch. Not surprising, I think I have finally experienced what's known as a "crash." The letdown following a prolonged adrenaline rush combined with an accumulated sleep deficit. I could barely get out of bed this weekend.

The good news is that I am starting to get some flexibility back in my foot...though I don't think it's as much as Kim's. My challenge to her, only half joking, is that at her current pace, she should start walking before me. I know already that she's currently running a spiritual and emotional marathon.

THE GRINDER

Claude Sidi was our dentist who was also a good friend. He moved mountains when he was able to replace the teeth your mother had lost in the accident. Dr. Sidi didn't have privileges at your mother's hospital, and there was no way we could bring her to his office in San Francisco for the procedure. Therefore, Claude decided he could be a little sneaky and do it after hours right in your mother's hospital room.

"Clandestine Claude's" performance began at 10:00 PM, under the cover of darkness when your mother's roommate, Mrs. Thompson, had fallen into a good, deep sleep. Thankfully, Mrs. Thompson was not easily roused, and she enjoyed sleeping the way a Ferrari likes to go fast.

Your mother and I found great amusement in the very nature of Claude's clandestine mission. We thought it was hilarious that he had to sneak around the hospital, trying to avoid detection by the vigilant nurses, the guardians of protocol. It would have been a serious offense for Claude, had he been caught, but your mother and I relished any situation where we could find humor, and we liked the idea that we were bending the rules just a little bit. No harm, no foul – as long as we didn't wake up Mrs. Thompson.

Your mother and I were already grinning when Claude entered the room. It didn't take us long to start laughing when we saw his giant toolbox. "Good lord," I exclaimed, "what on earth do you have in that thing?"

"Hey, man," Claude replied seriously, "this is my traveling office. Check it out."

Sure enough, he had packed in that box just about everything except his dental hygienist and x-ray machine. The first thing he did was to put on his head what looked like a fancy coal-miner's lamp. He then switched on the lamp, as it was dark in our room. He looked slightly ridiculous and we couldn't help laugh at his illuminating presence. He then stopped and looked around.

"What's wrong?" I asked.

"I need an outlet," Claude replied seriously. "It's time for power tools."

Claude reached into his box and pulled something out and held it loftily above his head as if he had sole possession of Excalibur itself. He held it up even higher and pressed a button. It was "The Grinder."

"Rrrreeeeeennnnggg!" whined the little electric Excalibur.

"My Gaaawd!" I whispered above my own laughter. "That thing is louder than hell!"

"I hope it doesn't wake Mrs. Thompson," replied Claude coolly, who suddenly looked a lot more like a vigilant Clint Eastwood than some devious dentist.

"Why don't you use that thing to cut a hole in wall and get us out of here," I said, still in disbelief. Claude then reached back in his box and pulled out a pair of safety glasses with a little magnifying lens that swiveled down over one eye. Your mother and I both cracked up when we saw it. Claude had transformed into some kind of demented, mad scientist from a James Bond movie, whose weapon of mass destruction – a tiny spinning wheel on top of a stick – was capable of blowing out eardrums.

"Rrreeeenngg…Rrrreeeeeeeeeennnggg," screamed the Grinder. We thought that Mrs. Thompson would surely wake up to this screeching high-speed diamond blade cutter that sounded as if it were slashing through concrete that was alive and screaming in agony.

"Stop it," he implored, "you're interfering with my work!"

"No, your art," your mother corrected.

"Open wide," commanded Claude, now trying to contain his laughter. "Now bite down …"

"Rrreenngg. Rreengg! Rrrreeeeeeeeeeeeeennnnngggggg!"

Surely, if Excalibur didn't wake Mrs. Thompson from her slumber, the three lunatics laughing hysterically in her room should have.

In the end, along with the new temporary tooth for your mother, Claude gave us the best medicine ever: side-splitting laughter. Poor Mrs. Thompson missed all the fun.

Not all business relationships were also personally rewarding. If we had to choose, why not do business with those we knew and liked? Business, as Dr. Sidi exemplified, was a lot more than just chasing the dollar. It was sometimes about moving mountains...for and with those we wanted to help anyway.

In the topographical shift that resulted from our moved mountain, we probably created rivers and streams with our tears of thanks and joy to the many people, such as Claude, who moved mountains on our behalf. No bulldozers were needed. Just big hearts.

SLEEPLESS NIGHTS

In my world, most experts argued that parents should avoid picking up their crying babies at night. But I couldn't help it. I remember one particular night, during an especially dark period, shortly after the accident, I needed to hold you more than you needed to be held by me. Picking you up may not have been the best thing for you, but it felt like the best thing for me.

You allowed me to cry, which I didn't often do. Truthfully, there were many times when crying was somewhat selfish. The hurt or pain was *my* hurt or pain, and my tears were for what *I* had lost. On this particular night, however, my tears were for your mother. I thought about how much she had lost. It was such a killer. During the day, I had experienced such joy playing with you on the floor, but your mother could only watch. She was delighted that you and I could play together, but I knew how devastating it was for her to not be able to partake in that simple pleasure...one that every parent normally took part in.

Sure, there were times that my tears were selfishly focused on my own pain, discomfort, burdens, worries, etc. That night, especially, my tears were for your mother. It broke my heart that she could not enjoy her daughter through some of the simple things like romping on the floor. Or sharing a bath. Or walking down the street with you in your stroller.

DEC 8, 2002

TU KNEW...TUNU?

Here in the hospital, things run a little differently. Getting our meals straight, for example, is a daily challenge. Every other day, a nutritionist comes by and attempts to take Kim's order for the next few meals. He is a very strange fellow named Tu.

Tu always makes us think of deer because his name is like that of "Tunu," which is an ancient Peruvian name that, roughly translated, means "a young male deer thinking about going to hunt for wild onions." We found that name hilarious, which is how we found Tu, even though he hasn't been able to give Kim the meal she ordered in the five weeks we've known him.

It's become a running joke and we look forward to Tu's visits so we can give him a hard time. We think he enjoys it as well and we've finally reasoned that, as the meals are so horrible anyway, the laughter provides far greater therapeutic value than any perceived nutritional benefits from even correctly delivered meals.

Tu is a very strange fellow, and Kim and I have reasoned that the only way he can keep his job is because he amuses his supervisor much the same way he amuses us. We cannot, for the life of us, understand a word he says and, obviously, he can't understand us either. He speaks really fast and has an accent whose origin is not locatable. His native tongue might be from a lost language, or perhaps, he developed his own language in order to be unintelligible.

We give Tu a hard time, but in an endearing and loving way. We all laugh openly (even Tu) during order-taking time so we figure it is good medicine for everyone. For example, Kim hates eggs. Every time, Tu asks her if she wants eggs for breakfast. "No, Tu," Kim says, "no eggs!"

"Oh yes," he replies, "no eggie. Yeah, right. Got it." Nevertheless, Kim gets eggs practically every morning. Sadly, we might be Tu's only friends. We don't mind at all because we're all slightly nuts.

Meanwhile, not far away, near the Ahrens-Hudson compound in Cupertino, things are also a little different. Wild deer roam the hills looking for ripe berries, tender morsels of shrubbery, and small dogs to attack. At first, we found the resident deer near us to be cute and, well...endearing. Later, we learned that they are also slightly nuts. (Yes, we must be in California.) Our neighbor, Mr. Randall, owns most of the mountain and has some realistic bronze deer statues in front of his house.

One morning, he mentioned that the bronze on one of the statues had weathered quite differently than the others. This had been a mystery for quite a while. Then, one day he looked out his window early one morning and saw a live resident deer mounting the bronze doe statue in his front yard. Weathering mystery solved, and wacky deer discovered.

Mr. Randall also informed us that the deer have been known to chase cars going up the hill and have, on occasion, been seen attacking coyotes, presumably over property rights and access to fresh game. No wonder our dog Sparky (a smart but aggressive

Jack Russell Terrier) cowers in fear when she confronts the snarling, territorial, meat-eating, and sex-crazed deer on our hill.

As we neared your mother's discharge date, her case manager informed us that our insurance company had refused to provide coverage for an outpatient rehabilitation program. I was outraged. This was more than a simple oversight because your mother's accelerated discharge date was conditional upon her receiving outside rehabilitation, to which our insurance carrier had previously agreed. They had asked us to take a compromised form of care (at-home versus in a clinic or hospital), to which we readily agreed. It was costly for the insurer and definitely more appealing to us than staying or traveling elsewhere. Then we were denied that as well.

The advance notice for this terrific news was less than a week before your mother's proposed discharge. It was actually much better, I later learned, than what most patients received, which is usually the day before they were thrown out onto the street. Your mother was, obviously, more than slightly disappointed. All we could do upon hearing this bombshell was just sit there, silently dumbfounded: lost in our swirling emotional cocktail of shock, outrage, dismay, and contempt.

Then, 15 minutes after our meeting, we witnessed the miracle of miracles: our case manager ran up to us and said, gleefully, that our insurance had reversed its decision and would, after all, cover two weeks of outpatient rehabilitation. We were incredibly relieved. Nevertheless, it was not without a cost. Your mother's brief in-home rehabilitation care would be covered if we agreed to relinquish potential other benefits for which we would normally be eligible. I quickly weighed the probabilities and chose the coverage that would help your mother right then, when she needed it. Witnessing our insurance carrier expose its underside with such obvious sleight of hand made me disgusted that a company in the service of "health-care" treated its customers so callously. And this was a very minor example of the abuses perpetuated by the System.

DEPARTURE – STAR DATE: 12.22.02

TOO MANY TWOS (TU'S?)...TOO MANY DAYS (DAZE)

Tomorrow we set sail and depart from this zany place called "Rehab." Given that our situation turned somewhat surreal a few months ago, it would be too uncomfortable if the rehab center were normal and rational. When you're slightly nuts, it's easier to navigate when your environment is even nuttier. At least that's our reasoning.

It is hard to believe that Kim returns home tomorrow. For a while, it seemed like that day would never come. Now that it's upon us, we are all filled with a rainbow of emotions. The first of which is Joy, of course, because the truth of her survival and vibrant life will be that much more of a reality to us. Relief, also, that she was able to survive not just the accident, but also the physical exhaustion of rehab and the mental strain of living in a hospital.

But for all our excitement, we are just a little nervous. Kim's care will now fall squarely on our shoulders. Outside the controlled environment of the hospital and back in the real world, where nurse call-buttons do not exist...but where, at home, love is far greater comfort. We will surely make our mistakes as we stumble along, but at least we get to make them together and adjust as we move forward.

Ironically, as we are so eager to leave the hospital, there are many desperate to get in. We hear the thumping of helicopter blades overhead, rushing to the hospital, and we know that someone is hoping to be saved. We always offer up prayers to those people and their loved ones.

For some, life is too painful or too difficult. Lord knows, we all have our worries and burdens. Among the many lessons we have learned from this little adventure is that there is always someone who has it worse and that, if we look just a little bit past our own noses, we get a glimpse of how blessed we really are.

SOUL SURVIVAL

I was at the center of this storm and trying to keep it all together, trying to shield you and your mother from my own tensions and frustrations, caused by the circumstances of our situation and fueled by the Tormentor within me. I wanted to protect you, but it took a toll on my own ability to keep it together. And I could not do it all by myself.

The only way I kept from getting completely unwound and unglued was by throwing myself at God's feet. I had to give in Him completely and relinquish what little control I thought I had. To confess that my only true strength was in the weakness I so meekly embraced. To not be embarrassed or ashamed of my weakness, but to somehow rejoice in it because that was where God would meet me. To let Him become all I needed when I realized that He was all I had.

When we pierced the veil, I took on the cloak of a new role. Along with my other roles, I became a caregiver. Just like your mother had to adapt to her new life in a wheelchair, I had to adapt to my new role.

To be sure, there were numerous challenges, from the simple to the strange and the surreal. More often, challenges become exaggerated because the situation was, at its most elemental level, simply *inconvenient*. Things took longer, and being a caregiver required primarily giving of my time to your mother in order to help and assist her.

The truth was that being a caregiver was hard work. It could be physically and emotionally draining. Most of us in my world were not trained or prepared to care for another person who was neither infant nor elder. I was not wired for that. My programming in life did not include such a variable, and most critically obvious, my schedule at the time did not allow room for the new routine. Very real tension was created when I tried to force the new and unforeseen requirements of care giving into an already busy life.

That tension was really heightened when my duties were performed with a hurried, expeditious or even exasperated attitude. Instead, I realized, they needed to be carried out patiently, with a deliberateness that transcended the duties themselves. Such intentionality conveyed a sense of caring and love that, when perceived by your mother, was far more beneficial than the actual services I provided.

It was in those moments when healing occurred. It may not have been physical healing, but it was where our conscious minds connected to a visible form of love that occurred when I could tend to your mother in a selfless, caring way.

It got us closer to God because I think it was how He wanted us to act. It made me reflect on how Jesus was the ultimate model of one who served with caring and compassionate selflessness.

In such times, however, my Tormentor lurked especially close to my elbow or near my ankle. It hoped to prey upon the times when I felt hurried or frustrated in my role as caregiver. My Tormentor wanted me to feel like a reluctant recruit instead of a willing and joyful volunteer. Instead of allowing me to help your mother with the kindness, patience, and love that were healing for her and that brought the two of closer to each other and to God, my Tormentor used every tool at its disposal (mainly, my own selfishness) to make me agitated, disgruntled and distracted. My Tormentor's singular goal was to disconnect me from God...or to divert my attention back to the familiar safety of life in our prior state. My Tormentor wanted me to gaze not forward with faith, but backward with longing of things we once knew on the other side of the veil, now beyond our reach and so very far away.

The Care Team

The things that matter will always be with you.

O UR FIRST ENCOUNTER WITH THE CARE TEAM was while we were still in Denver. When we realized that we would be returning to California, it became apparent that our old house was not going to be a reasonable option. It was simply too far away from San Jose, where your mother's hospital was located. It would have been a major effort to visit your mother there, especially for your grandparents, who were not comfortable driving in larger cities, let alone the zany freeways of the Bay Area.

We wanted you to be able to visit your mother every day, but no one was thrilled about having to drive you in a car over such long distances. We had just had a bad experience involving a car, and we wanted to minimize any associated risk and anxiety as much as possible.

I knew nothing about the San Jose area, and I had the opportunity to investigate its various living alternatives. We were still in Denver, and I was tending to your mother and you, and just coping with survival logistics and how to get us all out of there alive and together. Your mother and I were confessed San Francisco "City

Snobs," which meant that we identified solely with the City and assumed a pompous posture of indifference toward the outlying areas, especially the suburbs. Accordingly, we knew San Francisco like the back of our hands, but knew practically nothing beyond its 47 square-mile boundaries.

I asked one of our friends to look into possible housing options for us down in the foreign territory south of the City. It was not exactly an easy task. First, the house needed to be fairly close to your mother's hospital. Second, it needed to be big enough to accommodate an expanded clan. Third, it needed to allow dogs (Duffy and Sparky were in tow). Fourth, it needed to be accessible for your mother upon her discharge. And, fifth, if possible, it needed to be quiet. A respite from the high-anxiety we would be experiencing as we monitored your mother's condition, took care of you, and coped with the numerous uncertainties ahead. Oh yes, and the house could not bankrupt us, not an insignificant detail in the hyper-inflated Bay Area real estate market.

Amazingly, the Care Team found a house that was extremely secluded and offered incredible views of Silicon Valley. The house was, indeed, a great respite from the worries of the day. There were some drawbacks, of course, the most significant being that the lease agreement prohibited dogs. That was more of a challenge than an inconvenience as we had started to like bending a few little rules. On the whole, we could not have asked for a better house for our particular situation.

The other way the Care Team really came through was in bringing us prepared meals. Our days were spent primarily at the hospital, either with your mother or in the waiting room. Each day was emotionally draining and the last thing any of us wanted to do was shuffle into the kitchen to prepare a meal that nobody was inspired to eat anyway. It was not that we weren't hungry; we just did not have much enthusiasm for food. Our enjoyment consisted primarily of going to see your mother and taking care of you. These were indeed joyful activities, but they also imparted to us an underlying somberness as we became more consciously aware of how much you and your mother had each been compromised, although in different ways. The enormity of this insight quieted our appetite.

The Care Team, however, provided an incredibly useful ministry to us by simply delivering at our doorstep a few days' worth of prepared meals. Each meal came complete with labeled contents, instructions and any information – even a personal note – that the preparer wanted to include. The Care Team embodied an old maxim that my grandfather used to tell me over and over, "Many hands make light work."

I am still astounded when I reflect on how incredibly kind and supportive our family and friends were following our accident. Collectively and individually, they were the definition of compassion, which I defined as "love in action." Even now, after so many years, I am overwhelmed by how people gave of themselves to help us – you, your mother, and me.

Your grandparents, especially, were amazing in their selfless support of us. They stayed with us for months at our makeshift compound in California despite the stress and inconvenience of living in temporary housing and being away from their friends. Your grandmothers did the work of an army to help manage the household. They never complained at all when their backs and knees flared up from all the housework they did. Oh yes, playing with you probably contributed somewhat – you were starting to crawl, and keeping up with you required constant attention and supernatural stamina.

Their primary job was to look after you while your mother and I were recovering.

Your grandfathers did other kinds of work to help lighten our load. Your mother's father was an engineer and was always tinkering with things so that they worked better. My father secured provisions and did all kinds of thoughtful things for us. He also had a bad foot that needed surgery, but he bravely committed to having the procedure performed in California as opposed to near his home in Connecticut.

HOME SALE PREPARATION

The Care Team was mobilized again when we realized that we would need to sell our house in San Francisco. The house could not be modified to accommodate your mother's condition, and the hills alone in our neighborhood would have been a daunting challenge. Additionally, it was too far away from all of your mother's critical healthcare and rehabilitation providers. The accident had essentially caused our entire ecosystem to be transplanted from San Francisco to San Jose.

I was unable to manage the process and logistics of our home sale because I was too far away geographically, yet much too close emotionally. Furthermore, my plate was full just trying to restore some order to our lives that had turned chaotic. Therefore, I gave the Care Team carte blanche to do whatever they thought appropriate to get the job done. Of course, before the accident, your mother and I had not been planning to sell our house, and we were still trying to get our bearings straight as new parents. After the accident, we were in no way prepared to sort out which belongings to keep, which ones to put in storage, and which ones to give away or sell.

My mental capacities were far too compromised to make such arduous, if not momentous, decisions.

More truthfully, I really didn't care. Our belongings and other assorted stuff and things meant very little to me now. The easiest solution would have been to either toss it all in the Bay or, more appropriately, drop it all off at the nearest Goodwill store. I had no need for most of it, and that which I did need could be replaced. Most "stuff" just got in the way – it cluttered the mind as well as the closet. Therefore, I told the Care Team to have at it and do whatever they thought was best. Of course, they packed it all.

I made an in-person appearance during the final pack-up of our belongings. I was wearing a walking cast to support my foot and ankle. Getting up the front steps of our entrance walkway was more difficult than I had imagined. Before the accident, I had been in pretty good shape, going up and down those hills, but I was surprised at how quickly my leg muscles had atrophied. I found strange solace in this newfound realization that it hadn't been just my mind that had withered.

I entered the house and greeted a multitude of friends who had given up a beautiful Saturday in order to pack up our belongings. I was really touched. It was a party, of sorts, as people felt like they were really doing something positive and helpful, which they were. It was great to see so many friends in one place instead of the quick, isolated visits our crazy schedules usually limited us to. I wished, desperately, that your mother could have been with me.

I quickly realized, however, that this scene would have killed her. It would have broken her heart. Not so much that we had to leave our house, but that we had to do so on terms other than our own...and under such a traumatic cloud. I don't know what would have been worse: to say farewell to the house while watching our friends dismantle it, or to not say good-bye at all physically, yet keep our memory of it intact, the way we would want to remember it. Yet, as I looked around, all the various items that our friends were boxing up seemed so insignificant and valueless. I was appalled that I had once treasured some of these things that now seemed so trivial. The house and the memories it contained were precious; the assorted items within represented excess baggage that I neither needed nor wanted.

Your mother never again went inside that house. She remembered it just like we left it, the day we departed for a quick weekend trip to Denver. She never got to say good-bye. I, on the other hand, got the chance to bid farewell, but not how I would have wished. I took one last tour, slowly hobbling from room to room, saying a eulogy to each one as I passed through it. I was doing it for your mother, and for our dogs, and for me. And, of course, for you. This was supposed to the home you grew up in. As I walked through it, the house was so empty, so hollow and lifeless. At that moment, I felt exactly the same.

I went upstairs and tried to admire the living room we had enjoyed so much. It was barren, except for the echo in my mind of how the room used to be. Impulsively, I then turned around and looked up at your mother's loft. It, too, was barren and vacant. But I could see your mother coming down the spiral staircase, as nimble as before, jumping off the final step with a childlike joy she'd never let go of. She disappeared from my vision as my eyes fixated on that spiral staircase. I thought about how hard it now was for her to do even the simplest tasks that she used to take for granted. I thought about how wounded her body was, and yet how resilient and strong her mind and spirit were. I was so proud of your mother because she gathered strength where she could find it. In contrast, I then felt a wave of shame because, though I was physically intact, my soul seemed so wounded.

I looked again at the staircase and at the iron railing going around and round. It reminded me of a snake climbing a tree. It further brought to mind other reptiles like alligators and...Dragons. I drew a deep breath as I felt my Tormentor stir inside me, obviously delighted that it was so close to both my body and mind. I was determinaed to prevent my Tormentor from having another bite out of my hide, so I turned around, went down the stairs and out the front door, where Walter was waiting patiently. My Tormentor had enjoyed many tasty nibbles at my expense. It had not earned this little snack, and I was not about to give it another free sample.

I reflected upon leaving our house for the final time, that it had been a dwelling where love flourished. That is what made it special for us. We had loved this house, as had the people who had lived in it before us. I was sad to leave our house because of the love it represented for us. I was heartened, however, by the belief that we could bring that foundational ingredient with us to wherever we might live, in whatever house we might dwell. That kind of home, I told myself, was highly transportable.

CHAPTER ELEVEN

REHAB BEGINS AT HOME

The only way out is through.

THE GOOD PEOPLE HELPING YOUR MOTHER'S REHABILITATION at Valley Medical Center kept drilling in us the notion that, "rehab begins at home." At first, I thought it was their attempt to disclaim responsibility for any mishaps or unforeseen challenges that we might encounter the second we left their premises. After we pierced the veil, we began to see how universally accurate that statement became. It was analogous to any sporting event: you cannot get game ready without getting into the game.

Your mother's rehab facility (and most hospitals, for that matter) was built and equipped specifically for people with physical limitations. These facilities were deliberately protective. Everywhere, there were extra-wide hallways and doorways; big, accessible bathrooms with roll-in showers; stand-alone, low-rise sinks that were easy to reach and roll under; counters at a lower, more appropriate height; and a staff of trained professionals to provide assistance with just about anything. Everything was designed to help make patients well enough to go home.

Going home entailed a whole new dimension of rehabilitation that a hospital could not begin to approximate. It was kind of like a small group of kids playing sandlot baseball suddenly being thrust into Yankee Stadium to play against the Bronx Bombers. Or, more aptly, learning how to swim in the lovely, heated pool at the country club, under the watchful eye of a trained life-guard, and then suddenly being transported in full SCUBA diving gear down 60 feet underwater along the Great Barrier Reef, swarming with Great White sharks. Without the benefit of having had SCUBA diving lessons.

After we pierced the veil and your mother was in a wheelchair, rehab at home began at the front door. We hoped it would be wide enough to allow us to get in the house. We hoped the threshold didn't include too many steps. Before we pierced the veil, we never paid much attention to things such as door widths and thresholds.

Once we got inside, we hoped that the hallways would be wide enough and that the corners weren't too tight to get around. We realized that our bedroom was going to be a little crowded and that the bed would need to be moved in order to accommodate the wheelchair that had to go next to one of the sides. We thanked God that we did not need a lift for your mother to transfer from her wheelchair onto the bed. But then we realized that the height of our bed needed to be adjusted. In fact, we actually needed a new bed. We wondered what other kind of new furniture or equipment we would need.

Our bathroom needs were different after we pierced the veil. Your mother's body had been compromised, and thus, it functioned differently than before. Things didn't just happen as automatically as they used to. There needed to be regular intervention and, often, special equipment. Our bathroom, like most, was incapable of servicing someone in a wheelchair. Your mother couldn't even get in the bathroom to wash her hands because the doorway was not wide enough to allow her wheelchair to pass through.

My mind began to scan over all the other possible obstacles we might come across…things we had previously always taken for granted. What about bathing? Was the bath or shower accessible? Probably not. That would mean another alteration, modification, or new equipment purchase.

What about getting around the house in general? I didn't want your mother to be a prisoner in her own home. Was the living room or dining room sunken, with steps down? What about the kitchen? It was going to be tough for your mother to maneuver in there, as well. Your mother loved to cook and just be in the kitchen. It would be nice for her to be comfortable in the heart of our house, without feeling like she was in the way or a burden to others preparing the meals.

I was anxious about going home. It seemed like there were millions of considerations we needed to address in order to make your mother feel welcome and not captive. Would she be a prisoner of a room in the house? What about going outside? What about the steps? How easy was it to open and close the doors? Would all this require assistance, or could your mother navigate some of this independently? How much work needed to be done to make it accessible and livable? Were the telephones accessible? Should we make an eyehole in the front door at a level so that your mother could determine the identity of someone outside?

What about transportation and getting around? Would your mother be able to independently operate a vehicle? How would we find out? Where did such a vehicle come from? How much would it cost? Who would maintain and service such things?

When we pierced the veil, we returned home with a new outlook…and new things to look out for. We started to quickly realize how much easier certain things had been in the hospital. At home, we were suddenly more on our own than we wanted to be.

Rehab at home also implied and encompassed all the ordinary daily activities that now had to be undertaken without the help of hospital staff. Helping your mother turn in bed was a critically important activity. After we pierced the veil, we realized that able bodies turned automatically during sleep as a way to prevent skin sores. For your mother, turning in bed was no longer automatic, and it was definitely not easy. We knew that if she did not turn in bed on a regular basis, she would get skin sores. If undetected, skin sores could become dangerously infected and result in possible amputation or a sudden, uncontrollable rise in blood pressure (known as Autonomic Dysreflexia), which could be fatal.

After we had pierced the veil, we realized that the road to recovery – to increased independence – often required a *dependence* on others. It was not easy for your mother or me to enter into such a relationship. There were some things that I did willingly and lovingly. Others were more challenging, sometimes physically... usually emotionally. Some things were awkward and unpleasant. Some things brought us great joy and brought us closer together. We realized that rehab at home simply meant learning how to get on with our lives.

A critically important lesson we learned along the way was that the anger and frustration, which could easily arise, were not due to the person but rather due to the situation. We learned that our new life involved not just better awareness and management of our personal relationships with God, others, and ourselves but that it also meant better awareness of our situation or predicament.

JANUARY 27, 2003

"THE ONLY THING WE HAVE TO FEAR IS...FEAR ITSELF"

Franklin D. Roosevelt's rallying cry for the U.S. to officially engage in World War II is perhaps my favorite quote of all time. It became my personal rallying cry soon after our accident. My simple interpretation is that you gotta have faith. Faith in God, in yourself, in your friends, family, and colleagues, and in the belief that the future will ultimately be better than the present. This trust is the manifestation of God's Grace.

Ultimately, we need not fear anything because God has taken care of everything. That doesn't mean we shouldn't shuffle our feet and work hard at every endeavor; rather, it simply implies that we needn't fear so much the present outcome, because the ultimate outcome is assured. It's all in God's control, which means that the outcome is going to be good. Should we be fearful, we had better be afraid, because it means we have lost our faith.

Rehab at home meant that we had to contend with our pain and discomfort. Pain attempted to draw our attention to itself alone at the expense of all else. Pain wanted to separate us from everything else we knew so that it could have exclusive domination over us. Pain was the Tormentor's weapon of choice because it tried to separate us from all we knew and trusted. The Tormentor's goal was to isolate us and to separate us from Grace, thereby arousing in us any fear it could. Pain and fear were allies. Each on its own was dangerous; together they could be deadly.

After getting somewhat settled in our rented house in Cupertino, I finally had time to turn my attention to our abandoned home in San Francisco: the one we had lived in when you were born, the one we had left when flying off for a weekend in Denver. It was obvious that we would never live in that house again. It was a funky Victorian set on the side of a hill in a part of San Francisco that actually had decent weather. We loved that house.

I remember the first time your mother and I walked through the house. It was on a wet, rainy afternoon during a cold week in March. It was before we were married. The house was for sale, and we were "just looking." I wasn't really serious about buying anything, but I enjoyed looking at houses, especially interesting ones. This particular house had been built around 1900, therefore older than most houses in San Francisco that had been built since the Great Quake, and subsequent fires, of 1906. It was originally a very small house, but had been added to by prior owners such that its unusual layout gave the house an air of mystery and intrigue. The most interesting thing about this house, for us, was that as soon your mother and I entered the kitchen, we had a sudden flash of seeing our lives together in that house. We had been dating for two years, and I knew that we would be eventually getting married. I just didn't know exactly when I'd ask her the important question. Being together inside that house accelerated the process. I proposed to your mother a few days later.

It was a painful realization that we would have to sell our home after the accident. It was gut wrenching. Especially given the circumstances in which we had to sell it. Your mother and I discussed whether it would even be possible to try to make it accessible for her in a wheelchair. I was the practical one, and she was the one with faith and vision, the one who encouraged me to "believe it, and then you'll see it." Try as I may, I just couldn't figure out how we could possibly reconfigure our house to suit our new needs.

I visualized the house and its quirky features. I began to see that many of the things that we had found so endearing about our house were now obstacles that would be almost cruel in our new condition. I saw the sloped driveway going into a carport that was so narrow that we had to get real skinny just to squeeze in and out of the car. I saw the narrow steps from our sunken carport going up to the front door. I loved these steps because they looked right in the kitchen window, where you could see what your mother was cooking... and usually smell it. I kept thinking: How could she possibly get up those steps? They were way too steep to make a ramp practical and there was no way to make them wider.

I thought about the other entrance, the one coming into the front door from the sidewalk. The house was on a steep hill; so going through our entrance walkway was never easy, even for fully able-bodied people. My mind told me that it could be modified, however, with some creative concrete ramping. I kept encouraging myself, thinking: The front door is definitely wide enough! And the kitchen and dining room would need only slight adjustments! Hey, maybe this is doable!

Then I saw our master bedroom...and my heart sank. Our bedroom was on the first floor, which was great, but it required going through a doorway, up a small flight of steps, where a bathroom area was, then a step down to get into the bedroom. Oh, how brutal.

I then took a mental tour of other parts of the house in order to explore or create other potential possibilities. I saw the stairway going upstairs. I saw it and stared at the first step. I was afraid to move my eyes and go up any further. I thought of your mother not being able to walk up these stairs anymore. God, how I wished it had been me instead of her.

My mind couldn't take me up those stairs. Instead, I pictured an elevator there. It would never work in real life, but I visualized one just so that I could get my mind beyond the stairwell and up to the second floor. This floor was a little bit more accessible. Your room was actually quite easy and the living room, our favorite room, was big and open. This would be a great room for your mother! I thought to myself. We had always loved this room. It was a big room with tall, 20-foot ceilings and had giant windows from the old San Francisco Public Library that provided wonderful views of the Western Hills, whether casting shadows of the setting sun or being massaged by the fingers of incoming fog. It was a beautiful room.

I then looked behind me and saw our other guest bedroom. Also down a small flight of stairs. No way, I thought, this room won't work. God, what a bummer. I then looked forward and saw what I knew would be the worst: the spiral staircase leading up to your mother's loft. This was the way to your mother's little sanctuary. After we bought the house, we discussed where we might like to have our offices or private areas. I chose the basement. Your mother, knowing me all too well, said that she wasn't surprised, because my "heaviness" made me keep my head low and seek lower ground, where seriousness dwelt, as she liked to say.

Your mother, on the other hand, was delighted to get the loft. She had such "lightness" about her that she automatically gravitated to where there was more light, space, and air. The loft was her special area. It was the smallest "room" in the house but it was also the coziest, and because it had the highest vantage point, the loft had the best views from its corner windows. The only way to access it was by way of the skinny, 10-foot high, iron spiral staircase. At the top of the staircase, however, we had to duck our heads really low to avoid the big wooden beam that framed the loft's entrance.

I remember going up that staircase countless times, either to see your mother or just admire the view. More times than not, I hit my head on that stupid beam. Your mother always reprimanded me because I typically hit my head on lots of things. She reminded me that I was always looking down, not up.

"Think light," your mother would say encouragingly, "don't let your head and shoulders get so heavy that they pull you down. How can you see God, let alone where you're going, if you don't look up?"

I then looked up at the spiral staircase, the one your mother used to go up and down several times a day...habitually, without thinking. Because of the accident, she never got to do it again. I looked further up, not enjoying the image any longer...and I didn't see God. I looked down at the floor. The sight of my walking cast made me feel embarrassed that my injury was so insignificant compared to your mother's. It didn't seem fair. I don't know how long I just stood there, not believing it. Why did it have to be her? Why couldn't I be the one in the wheelchair? I was the strong one; it should have been me.

My heart grew heavy, and it groaned under the weight of its accumulated sorrow. I had to snap out of it and pull myself out of a worsening funk. I then realized that I wasn't as strong as I had thought I was. Sure, I was physically stronger than your mother, but she was stronger – and tougher – mentally, emotionally, and spiritually. This realization gave me a small measure of comforting reassurance that we would be all right. Your mother was strong enough in the areas where it mattered most. The very qualities that made me love her so. Love was at the foundation of it all.

We had put so much love and work into this house in making it our home. We loved being there, and it became a reflection of our personalities. When we knew you were coming, we made over one of the guest rooms and turned it into your nursery. It was beautiful. You had the best room in the house. I remember painting it when we first moved in, transforming the light blue walls into a more soothing Tuscan Yellow. It was not an easy feat in that it required several coats of primer and paint. My ladder barely enabled me to reach the peak of the ceiling, some 15 feet high. Re-painting the room for your arrival, however, was a breeze by comparison, because you gave me some supernatural inspiration.

Over the ensuing months, your mother continued to progress in ways that astounded everyone who knew her. Those who knew her, of course, were not really surprised because your mother's courage and determination was truly remarkable. Nevertheless, given the severity of her injuries, her recovery was astounding. And inspiring.

For example, she got to the point where she was cooking meals in the kitchen on a regular basis. She could maneuver around the house with complete independence and could even do everything required to take care of you. There were times when I traveled for business. Early on, we would arrange for a friend or relative to stay over at our house while I was gone, just to make sure there were no accidents or to prevent potential mishaps. Eventually, your mother decided that she didn't want anyone staying over on those occasions when I had to be away. She wanted to feel fully independent, and she wanted the opportunity to be together with you without the distraction of another person. By every measure, she became fully independent.

Your mother began a regular routine of walking as a means of physical therapy and strength conditioning for her legs. She used a walker to help stand up from her wheelchair and then walked across the house and back. She especially liked to show off when we went over to a friend's house. She would navigate a few steps getting into the house and then walk right into the kitchen or dining room. It was an impressive sight that often caused eyes to get misty (especially mine), and it was more practical than hauling our heavy metal ramp over the steps to enable her wheelchair to access the house. Seeing your mother on her two feet made for a grand entrance. It also helped increase her self-esteem and self-confidence.

FEBRUARY 18, 2003

SEWING GREAT STRIDES

Extraordinary people do remarkable things but make them look rather ordinary. Or, some extraordinary people do ordinary things but in a remarkable fashion. One might not think an activity such as sewing to be particularly noteworthy, except when taken into account the remarkable dexterity and fine motor skills required to thread a needle and guide it deftly in a purposeful pattern. Before the accident, Kim engaged in all kinds of sewing projects, many of which I kidded her about as being somewhat old-fashioned. She would always counter with the notion that she was upholding the spirit of Old World artisans and honest craftsmanship. As a sensitive sort of guy, I could always appreciate the skill...I just could not quite tolerate the time – I am just way too impatient.

In any event, Kim's dexterity has improved so much that she was able to sew some hems on a couple of her pants! This is a huge development and one that is somewhat defiant of some physicians' prognostications. It is a result of lots of hard work on Kim's part, a refusal to acquiesce, and plenty of prayers.

If sewing is subtle, then walking is not. For months, Kim has been using a walker and, with it, has been "doing laps" around the hall and kitchen. It is hard work. It started off as a form of physical therapy and has been progressing steadily since. For example, the past couple of weeks, she has walked in and out of houses hosting her bible study group. The other night, Kim, Olivia and I went out to dinner, and Kim walked in and out by herself. It was fantastic! She is such a trooper and such a champion. Her progress has been so amazing, that it seemed quite natural when she did it. But as I reflect on it now, while writing this, it hits me like a hammer just how much we have been through. And where we have come from. And how blessed we are.

In case it's not already obvious, I was a big believer in getting as much capable help as possible. It is primarily because I didn't ask for enough help that I am now so passionate about how important it can be to your health and the health of those around you. It may also influence how much people enjoy being around you.

Part of the reason I didn't ask for enough help is that I felt overwhelmed from the outset. Things were happening so fast that I found it difficult to say, "Time Out," and stop to restructure things. The other reason is that I was experiencing our new world for the first time; everything was completely new and foreign to me. My old operating manual was useless. I wasn't even aware of the things I would need to know about. I didn't know what I didn't know.

As we emerged from the urgency of survival, the migration toward recovery was tricky. Recovery took much longer than survival. There were many demanding issues that kept lingering, and they conspired to steal as much as possible from our quality of life. Especially at risk was my health.

Even in recovery, your health and wellness can easily become compromised or neglected when the world begins to rush in on you and you can't react quickly enough to everything vying for your attention. Therefore, as soon as you can, begin or commit to an exercise program.

The first thing to remember is to breathe. As in very slowly... B-R-E-A-T-H-E. Taking in oxygen is literally inspiring (just like dying is literally expiring). Eat smart. Try to rest. Stress is high, the demands are intense, and the road to burnout is fast and straight. Caregivers, especially, need to take care of themselves because nobody else can do it for them. They can help others only if they themselves are in good shape physically, emotionally, and spiritually.

I was living proof of the perils of neglect. I had a poor diet, was unable or unwilling to exercise, hardly slept, and tolerated way too much stress. Consequently, I had to contend with a threatening heart condition. I could feel the stress building, but thought I was tough enough and strong enough to handle it. Guess again. A stress fracture is often very small and practically undetectable. But it inevitably grows and expands. Just like a buried emotion.

Nevertheless, I was also a big believer in the intangible health benefits of things like beer, cigars, donuts, and chicken-fried steak. Every year, for example, I attended an annual guys' weekend in Texas during which time we avoid all contact with all vegetables other than onions and potatoes. The goal was, naturally, to consume as much red meat as possible while avoiding a complete gastrointestinal traffic jam and/or total arterial meltdown.

We had learned a few things over the years that proved helpful in making for enjoyable weekends and that kept us in "fighting shape." The most obvious was to make sure to keep plenty of beer on hand. Beer helped such highly caloric food go down easier and provided a gentle effervescence in the stomach that acted as a soothing digestive agent. Meanwhile, the natural fiber in beer (barley and hops) helped to further clear away any clogged particles in both the digestive tract and within the bloodstream. It was amazing!

Another important trick was to make sure plenty of donuts and cinnamon rolls were on hand. These quick and easy "treats" were great "pick-me-ups" at any time of day and, conveniently, provided an excellent source for two of the basic food groups: flour and sugar.

A third consideration for a bountiful guys' weekend culinary fest was to incorporate a deep fryer in all the major meals. This was for men only. In my time, women had yet to simplify their dietary needs to the irreducible minimums that men had. For example, women still needed vegetables and other "appetizers" that could take up valuable refrigerator shelf space that could otherwise be used by meat and beer. Furthermore, a deep fryer was a piece of heavy equipment and needed to be operated by certified professionals. It was not something to be learned at home in the presence of children or small animals.

Some items lent themselves quite naturally to a deep fryer. Onions and potatoes, for example. Other things had taken years of sophisticated experimentation to discover the glory that could be unlocked from within the depths of the fryer. Hamburgers reached new heights after emerging from the fryer's nadir. Donuts (already cooked) were unfathomably delicious when re-fried. Cinnamon rolls, when given a deep-fried bath of bubble and boil, were allowed to blossom the way that their creator had intended.

In a nutshell, the deep fryer could send otherwise essential, yet simple, cuisine soaring to new heights of gastronomic ecstasy. Furthermore, as an added benefit, any remaining oil left over in the fryer could later be used as fuel for almost any motorized power tool. We even found that this oil dramatically improved the performance of Jet-Skis. Unfortunately, our scent attracted a trail of ravenous fish and other boaters, all of whom were drawn to the lingering essence of deep-fried goodness. The gathered crowd was far too great for our humble, modest group and it also made simple stunts on the Jet Ski nearly impossible.

The last consideration for a proper guy's weekend was to make sure to end every meal with a cigar. Those who were truly experienced knew that it was best to also begin every meal with a cigar. Especially breakfast.

I was not iconoclastic just for the sake of being different, but sometimes my sanity required that I had to break the routine. It was good for my mind and body to shake off potential complacency and live a little. Indulge a little...or take it to the edge. When I returned home, I realized how good I had it. And I vowed to live and eat a whole lot healthier going forward. Except during that breakaway weekend, when I allowed my body to consume the things my mind thought it wanted. So it was a nice little breather from the routine. And I returned home newly resolved to re-commit myself to being a whole lot healthier…in order to justify the next year's breakaway weekend.

THE ONLY WAY OUT OF THIS IS THROUGH

In my world, getting beyond the challenge of many of life's obstacles required a keen sense of direction. Hard-charging Teddy Roosevelt used to preach to his children "over, under or through, but never around." We learned that, to truly get beyond a challenging obstacle, we had to compromise its power and structure by going right through it. We would not necessarily kill the obstacle, and it wouldn't be rendered completely harmless, but it certainly would be compromised enough so that we could work our way through it. In the end, we would have triumphed, often more spiritually than physically.

When we went through something, there was a moment in which the obstacle became a part of us…we were briefly fused to one another. During that short time, our momentum would be naturally slowed down by the countervailing force and added weight that the obstacle imposed on us. Furthermore, we had to be prepared for a pivotal confrontation as we came face-to-face with our adversary. That was the moment of truth, because we definitely did not want to get stuck here. It required extra effort to keep on pushing despite the increased resistance coming from our nemesis. When we eventually made it through the obstacle to the other side, we experienced a subtle momentum shift: we were a little less crippled, and it was a little more so.

Such was the struggle I waged with my Tormentor. Although I had gone through it, it still continued to travel with me and nip at my heels in order to prevent me from truly, and peacefully, healing. It would roar in the evening and wake me from my slumber. My Tormentor seized every opportunity to disrupt my sleep and it turned my dreams into nightmares. It pursued me constantly and never let me out of its sights. It was relentless in trying to tempt me to give up. It was tireless…and I was not.

During the many dark moments while pushing through our obstacles, when we were slowed down and confronted by our tormentors face-to-face, we learned first-hand one of the most important lessons in our journey: that God did not necessarily deliver us *from* our troubles, but He did deliver us *in* our troubles. There was absolutely no way we could ever have gotten through our obstacles without leaning on God. It was what He wanted and it was what we needed.

No, I have not yet killed my Tormentor – because I cannot – but, with God's help, it is temporally incapacitated. But I still have to keep going; keep moving forward; keep focused on what's ahead and not the obstacles I have left behind. It is also why I am here with you, so that I may forewarn you of the perils that will surface should your world become shattered.

CHAPTER TWELVE

AUTONOMIC DYSREFLEXIA

We'll get them all eventually, so what would you like to lose first?
Your time, money, health, mind...

HEN WE PIERCED THE VEIL, WE LEARNED about all kinds of new diseases, illness, and conditions we had never before heard of. Most of them had unusual names, but some were easy to remember given the dangers they represented.

Among them, Autonomic Dysreflexia stood out. We had never heard of this condition before the accident, despite your mother's nursing background and medical training. Autonomic Dysreflexia was caused by an involuntary and uncontrollable rapid rise in blood pressure. This condition was practically unique to people with spinal cord injuries. It was dangerous because it could cause a stroke or heart attack.

Autonomic Dysreflexia could occur after an imbalance was caused in the internal body system, which controlled blood pressure. Such imbalances could be triggered by a painful stimulus, usually below the area of injury. When the "area of injury" was your neck, a large section of your body remained a vulnerable target. An obvious trigger was when the body became too hot. Another was the occurrence of a bladder or urinary tract infection (UTI), which, if left untreated, could cause a very nasty kidney infection as well as Autonomic Dysreflexia.

Unfortunately, it seemed that the major source causing Autonomic Dysreflexia was pain. Nerve pain was another common side effect for many people with spinal cord injuries. Some experienced little or moderate pain; others endured excruciating pain. Each case was different. Pain was so challenging because you could not see it. Nerve pain was particularly thorny because it was so elusive and difficult to treat effectively.

There were, of course, medications that could mask the pain, but they did not cure it. Some of these medications were very strong narcotics, which did indeed camouflage the pain, but they were insidious things that could blanket other sensations in life that were either enjoyable or necessary. These narcotics represented the ultimate compromise: if we *didn't* take them, then we would experience nerve pain; if we *did* take them, then we would experience nothing. They deluded us into thinking that we were in a natural state, but in actuality, they simply made us numb.

Nerve pain was simply dreadful. I had a little experience with it from my crushed foot, but nothing even close to what your mother experienced. Mine was limited to my foot and ankle. Hers encompassed much her entire body, even in areas where she didn't have complete tactile sensation, say, on parts of her legs. Her nerve pain was not that which was close to the surface of the skin; rather, it was deep within the core of her body and limbs. Nerve pain extended throughout her central nervous system.

Nerve pain was mysterious. Because every case was different, we did not fully know how it worked or what ignited it. Your mother and I learned, however, that her nerve pain was greatly influenced by emotional stress and anxiety. The fear and uncertainty that tormented her immediately after the accident greatly exacerbated the already severe pain of her fresh injuries. As she began to recover, and as we started to get more settled into a pattern of less chaotic, reactive living, her nerve pain intensified not by her own anxieties but by mine.

Your mother usually was very balanced and had an inner peace and calmness about her that I found truly wonderful and astonishing. While she could usually control her emotions, she couldn't always prevent them from hitting her far below the surface, where her nerve pain resided. Therefore, whenever I got visibly angry or frustrated (your mother called it "fussy"), her nerve pain would typically shoot through the roof.

This air of frustration created significant tension for us. I was often visibly tense, but then I would feel guilty because my own stress would cause your mother to feel anxious, which would, consequently, exacerbate her nerve pain. I was working hard trying to be a good provider; trying to manage all the new complications our new situation had thrown at us; trying to keep us moving forward physically, spiritually, and emotionally; and trying to be an attentive and loving parent and husband. I felt as though there was a mountain of demands – all of them urgent as well as important.

Nevertheless, my visible stress had the potential to literally kill your mother, and it created an unhealthy, toxic environment for you, a baby with already enough trauma in your young life. I decided to analyze all of my so-called demands and try to determine specifically which ones had the highest influence, or were most likely to cause my stress level to soar to an uncomfortable level.

The physical demands, such as increased work around the house, were significant but a necessary by-product of the accident. Besides, your mother was getting better and pitching in where she could, and of course, we could always bring in help if necessary. This was manageable.

The increased demands of parenthood, required due to some of your mother's limitations, were sometimes taxing, of course. However, I was getting an opportunity to spend increased time with you in a way that very few fathers from my world could. This, I realized, was much less a burden and much more of a blessing.

My work obligations, however, were indeed a challenge. Most careers in financial services were demanding and stressful. Investment banking, however, demanded significantly greater time, commitment, and sacrifice. The profession attracted people who were somewhat intelligent, highly motivated, and extraordinarily committed to success. (Consequently, we all suffered from a psychotic blend of massive ego and raging insecurity.)

In such a business, there was no way I could perform at a level even approaching minimum acceptable performance standards. But again, this was an unavoidable by-product from the accident. I would take my lumps in pride and compensation and be grateful that my firm was exceptionally supportive, patient, and understanding. Most other Wall Street firms would have likely sent me shuffling out the door as soon as I limped back in from the accident. No, I figured that I could learn to manage the stress from work.

That left essentially only one thing: the System. I finally realized what had been at the source of my growing sense of anger, frustration, and exasperation. The aggravations of dealing with the cruel practices and agonizing inefficiencies of the System were driving me crazy. The futility of achieving reasonable outcomes was maddening, and I was straining at every sinew to keep from blowing up.

Even more profound, the injustices that proliferated were both infuriating and heartbreaking. The System had become a network of conspiring businesses, all of which seemed to promote and perpetuate injustice in order to serve their own interests. Even more troubling was that all these entities were involved in the business of trying to help people, a cruel oxymoron.

Many of these companies became quite successful, but it came at a significant and tragic cost. Initially, that cost was incurred by their own individual customers, then gradually by a broader community, and then, ultimately, by our entire society. Health-related services became so profitable that the companies controlling their provision became models of inefficiency and financial malfeasance. It became a turning point in our country, which had previously championed the efficiencies and the resulting economic and societal benefits that could be achieved through a free enterprise model.

Our government had historically allowed private enterprises to provide essential services. The disaster of healthcare, however, illuminated the extent to which our social and economic infrastructure had transformed to the point where some services, once considered luxuries, had evolved into basic necessities. Thus, we felt that the delivery of such services was inappropriate for pure profit-oriented free market enterprises. Electricity, for example, was initially an expensive service available only to those who could afford such an exclusive item. It was later considered to be not a luxury but, rather, a basic necessity.

But not so for health insurance. Because it held the keys to health coverage, the health insurance industry did itself a disservice, in the eyes of society, by being so blatantly greedy while pretending to be a public servant. This disingenuous disguise eventually wore off and the hypocrisy of healthcare was exposed for all to see.

So now I think you begin to see that the primary source of my heightened stress was my entanglement with the System. I also learned along the way that we were not alone in our battle to stave off Autonomic Dysreflexia. Unwittingly, everyone in my world was in the grips of the System and engaged in a struggle for our sanity, if not our survival. I became so frustrated and furious that I thought my head would blow up. If I could have screamed loud enough, I'm sure it would have.

The System worked for some, but others with special needs situations had unique challenges. We were quite fortunate because your mother's condition improved dramatically from when we had the accident. She had recovered much more than many others with her level of injury whose disabilities remained severe.

Though some things definitely got easier, occasional challenges of our situation made me get anxious or sad or frustrated or angry. That's when the Dragon, my Tormentor, was most likely present. It fed on these little pangs of self-pity. Eventually, I learned to catch myself and stop such feelings before they ran too far because I realized just how fortunate we were compared to others for whom life was so much more difficult and for whom *everything* was a struggle.

APRIL 9, 2003

THE MOTHER SHIP

Among the many lessons I have learned in the "life is short" category is to vent quickly when I am frustrated and then try to forget the episode as quickly as possible. Don't hold a grudge or carry negative emotions beyond their point of utility. Correspondingly, because life is short, I get frustrated (okay, angry) when so many facets in our world are so incredibly inefficient or when people or systems are both inept and insensitive or immoral. Clearly, I am not politically correct. Nor do I intend to be. My definition of politics is the attempt to be wise without integrity.

Nevertheless, I hope you don't think that we are not grateful for what we have. Nothing could be further from the truth. Our gratitude list includes checkmarks in some of life's bigger boxes: a second chance at life, great families and friends, an amazing daughter, an opportunity to help others, and a chance for renewal and redemption. However, I get frustrated (okay, angry), when the bureaucracies or systems we must navigate through at present prevent us from embracing fully both what we have and what we need to do next. These things (legal, medical, insurance, real estate) consume an inordinate amount of time and energy that would otherwise be spent with family, friends, or, in our case, just plain healing and recovery. I think we all know which activities provide the greatest returns on invested time.

The unjust abuses of our time and sensibilities also try to rob us of what little time we do have with friends, family and healing. The negative energy from such abuses does not dissipate quickly but, rather, is prone to seep into the realm where it can be harmful to those we love most.

I hate the moments when I later discover that I had been serving as a conduit for negative energy. I often find it difficult to differentiate between anger and exhaustion-fueled frustration. Then, exasperation can become confused with ennui or being so accustomed to otherwise intolerable situations, that I am jaded or have otherwise resigned myself to accept whatever it is that common sense would not tolerate.

It is on the "light side" is where we find healing, joy and great prosperity of spirit. Forces from the "dark side," however, do in fact conspire to steal away our focus and energy away from those things that provide truth, meaning and goodness.

Finally, some of you have asked me about the Mother Ship. For me, the Mother Ship can mean several things: Heaven, corporate headquarters, or an insane asylum, to name a few. But it is also a real machine of transport. Some the rooms at our current compound, including our bedroom, overlook a wonderful valley, on the other side of which is a rock quarry belonging to the old Kaiser Company (which created Kaiser Permanente, the innovative HMO here in California). I have anointed one of the structures in the quarry complex as "the Mother Ship." It has a strange, mammoth dome-like shell that seems to sit atop steel pillars that look eerily like landing gear. When crews excavate in the mountain, dust kicks up, and sirens blare. I usually assume that the dome is preparing for lift-off. One of these days, I'll be right...just wait.

My pain hostility in response to the injustices of the System was, in my mind at least, certainly justified. Aggression, after all, was a form of self-preservation. But I was dangerously close to allowing these assaults on my sensibilities to create a near-fatal autonomic dysreflexic reaction. If that had happened, it was because I would have let the situations get the best of me. And I would have handed my Tormentor the cruel victory it was so intent on achieving.

CHAPTER THIRTEEN

THE SYSTEM

It kept us malnourished, even though we were its lifeblood.

*I*N MY TIME, WE WAGED A GLOBAL WAR against terrorism that we believed threatened our social and economic security. Terrorism constantly imperiled our sense of safety, security and independence. Notorious terrorists included al Qaida, the Taliban, Carlos the Jackal, Hezbollah, and Osama Bin Laden.

Nevertheless, the greatest threat to our country's welfare and prosperity was the economic and social terrorism from the enemy that lived within our own borders. It represented a far larger danger to our national wellbeing than any terrorist or imaginable weapon. It was our nation's health insurance system. The System had grown so out of control that it eventually held us hostage and demanded an incalculable ransom.

Instead of military incursions to fight terrorists in faraway countries, we should have invaded the System.

When we pierced the veil, we discovered that, in our world, there was no health or care in healthcare. The System of healthcare itself was sick. More seriously, what infuriated me the most about

125

the System was the underlying level of cruelty it perpetuated. The monolithic beast essentially hoarded our money and dictated the terms of care. Instead of serving as a conscientious steward, and administering assets and claims wisely and judiciously, the System denied reasonable service during those times when people had their greatest need.

If you were really sick or injured, health insurance companies did everything they could to make you even sicker. It was astonishing how far and wide they could cast their net of misery. I would ask my family, friends, neighbors, and co-workers to see how many had had positive experiences with their health insurance provider. The silence was deafening. So why were these guys in business?

The health insurance industry in our country grew from a small group of companies wanting to increase efficiencies into a massively complicated monolith that eventually impacted our entire economy. The System became so important that we ultimately allowed it to dictate our national policies and agendas. We became beholden to the System for almost everything. We would beg, and it would say, "No." It brought us to our knees, pleading and praying. It was pathetic.

Contrary to popular belief at the time, the quality of healthcare in America was not bad. In fact, it was great. We had the best facilities, technologies, and an army of highly trained, educated, dedicated and compassionate practitioners. What these people did, and the quality of care usually provided, was extraordinary. The problem with healthcare, therefore, lay within the System. And the System was controlled by insurance.

Insurance controlled the pre-care and after-care service. This service was, on the whole, atrocious, appalling and disgraceful. It limited who gained access based on participation in a company large enough to provide group coverage. Others could gain access, but at highly inflated admissions charges. There was a misalignment of interests, none of which benefited us as consumers. The System did everything in its power to create disincentives for seeking medical treatment by placing more of the burden of cost and procurement on us – its customers. Then, it employed strange, unusual and outright ludicrous tactics all designed to deny, delay and avoid any coverage or payment.

Because the System took more than it gave, denial became commonplace in our lives. As a result, medical practitioners frequently determined their medical treatment based on what a patient's insurance company would cover. Doctors were usually denied their desired treatment plan, so they had to be creative. Patients had little choice but to accept and acquiesce. In other words, insurance companies dictated medical care.

Compounding the denial and limited service options was the aggravation caused by the insane amount of time required to get anything done within the System's labyrinthine walls. Telephones were answered by automated attendants, who required that we answer a series of questions to help direct our call to the most appropriate department. After our calls were routed to that department, a representative would get on the phone and then require us to repeat all the information that we had supplied the automated attendant. Insurance company employees were generally kind, decent people who were working hard to support their families and climbing the ladder of the American Dream. Unfortunately, these people were employed by insurance companies principally to guard the Fortress. They essentially served as human shields to continually deflect us to someone else within the never-ending matrix.

The cruelty of the System, however, was not the fault of those customer service representatives, who guarded the Fortress and served as its first line of defense. Rather, it was senior management who orchestrated the rules of engagement the poor worker bees were ordered to carry out. Those poor drones on the front lines were disempowered of all practical means to act on behalf of any customer with whom they may have been interacting. They were simply phone messengers, serving as relay points that routed customers along to another layer within the matrix. Never up or through – always around or sideways.

Such people were usually genuinely sympathetic and would often confide that they would do more if they could, but that their hands were tied by the System. Unfortunately, there was strong incentive to keep it this way. Fewer payments made by preventing, denying, or delaying claims meant more money that was kept within the Fortress. This impressed investors, who nudged share prices continually higher, which resulted in a little bit more candy for those on the front lines who guarded the Fortress.

The entire operating protocol of the System was designed to waste as much of our time as possible so that we would eventually surrender our claim requests and simply pay out of pocket. Accordingly, this seemingly inefficient process was ruthlessly effective in reducing its claims payments, which resulted in increased profitability, higher stock market valuations and, thus, huge financial windfalls for their senior executives. It mattered not that it came at the expense of its own customers.

There was a very high inverse correlation between the amount of help an insurance company provided its customers and its profitability. This was corporate greed of the worst kind. I considered these organizations to be evil because the intentions behind their actions – or inactions – were often diametrically opposed to the companies' stated purpose of helping people in need.

It was stunning, the number of hours I spent while at work trying to rectify problems or issues that should have been immediately and automatically taken care of as a matter of course. What little productive time I had got gobbled up in dealing with these inane tasks. It was an outrageous waste of time.

In those dreary days, my mind easily concocted conspiracy theories. I therefore imagined that my insurance company sensed in me a good opportunity to receive higher premium dollars. Why? Because, as it continued to delay, confuse, and refuse all of my reimbursement claims, my carrier rightly assumed that my blood pressure was rising to unhealthy levels. Gee, Gil is a higher insurance risk; we better raise his rates. Of course, we won't cover any treatment for Gil's hypertension, because he should have taken better care of himself.

Most health insurance companies engaged in a practice of deferred maintenance that supported their philosophy that it was more profitable to pay for emergent care than to pay for care that might prevent an emergency. For many publicly traded companies, the near-term profitability that accrued from a policy of deferred maintenance was far too appealing to ignore. Virtually every management team wanted to avoid such costs as much as possible while on their watch; they simply passed those costs and responsibilities on to the next team. Ultimately, health insurers did not want to cover anything because, while their "service" was to help provide care and treatment to people who needed them, the insurers' *business* was to make as much money as possible, which required very stingy benefit coverage.

Such behavior was supported by Wall Street's maniacal desire to maximize short-term shareholder value. That goal was often best achieved by cutting costs wherever possible. Not coincidentally, of course, CEO compensation packages became based on near-term term performance measurements. Forget about doing the right thing that may have had more up-front costs but that reaped huge benefits for everyone in the long run. It was all about trying to increase positive cash flow in order to support or advance the company's stock price. Companies with the best share price performance were those that demonstrated consistent quarterly earnings and revenue growth. Companies did everything and anything necessary to maintain their quarterly growth momentum for fear of "disappointing" investors.

Many of those who could not afford to finance their own healthcare lived on the fringe of mainstream society. They were shunned and considered a detriment to their communities. They flocked to hospital emergency rooms for every medical concern – mild or severe – because they believed that hospitals had to uphold an oath to treat everyone.

Ultimately, however, our hospitals became so overrun with patients unable to pay for healthcare that the physicians and hospitals held a massive, nationwide strike. I am hazy on the details, but I seem to recall that the standoff included much anguish, torment, and even violence. Some hospitals closed down. Some attempted arson to collect fire insurance, which failed. And some transformed themselves into full-service pet salons. A few physicians stuck around, but most found better pay and job satisfaction as Elvis impersonators.

MAY 10, 2003

CRUTCH FREE

I hobble, limp, and gimp around and still need my removable walking cast to avoid dislodging some of that precious metal, but the crutches are gone. Those first few steps were a little scary, wondering if my foot could withstand full weight bearing. Was it up to the task? Was I? So it is with any crutch and our dependence on it.

I had become an expert on crutches and could cruise around faster than any ordinary pedestrian. Not surprisingly, I am much slower without them. It is a shocking reminder of how easy it is to get so dependent on our crutches, no matter their form. Life on crutches is harder at first, and then becomes comfortable when adapted to them. When those crutches are discarded, life without them is definitely harder at first before it becomes better...though not necessarily easier.

Of course, some of our crutches are necessary and most definitely appreciated. Our faith, families, friends, and therapies come to mind. But they each really entail a dynamic relationship that involves love and support that helps us grow, evolve, and transcend our current state. Most crutches help with where we are but don't offer much to get us beyond it. We just have to be mindful and vigilant against anything designed to initially help us, that later starts to hold us back – not due to its intent or limitations, but from our fearful reliance on it and reluctance to grow beyond it.

In fact, it is not even fair to imply that the people who have supported us are crutches because, in our state, we hardly had the strength to effectively lean on them. We were totally supported, which is beyond what a crutch is intended to do. Without a crutch, one gets by...just less efficiently. Without what we've received from all of you, we would certainly have perished. Really. You cannot imagine how much this has meant to us.

Going forward, it's all about attitude. Sometimes our determined, bullish attitude is incredibly abundant and seems unstoppable. At other times, the struggles and challenges are large and foreboding, and our attitude wilts and withers. It really is a day-by-day exercise of managing expectations and outcomes, and then giving thanks for what we have. But it thrills me to start living toward more days of crutch-free living. Or, at least leaning on the crutches of my choosing.

It is great to be rid of my walking crutches, but I know that other types remain that are not as easily discarded. Nevertheless, I know it's just a matter of time and attitude. To be sure, God's grace has lifted most of the crutches I thought I needed before the accident. How many, and which ones, I impose on myself from now on should prove interesting. But if we lean on each other, then the road ahead can only be rich and rewarding.

Now my life has changed in oh so many ways.

My independence seems to have vanished in the haze.

But every now and then I feel so insecure,

I know that I need you like I never did before.

(The Beatles – "Help!")

I became an expert at identifying people who were entangled in the System. It became scarily easy. For example, if I came across a grumpy person, it was highly likely that he or she had either just spent a long time on the phone with numerous Fortress-protecting bees, or had just met with someone else who had been. The resulting bad energy from such encounters was so easily transferred that it could spread faster than the Ebola virus.

In fact, the System *was* the Ebola virus of our times. The system was an air borne weapon of mass destruction. I began to believe that, if left unchecked, the System would quickly turn us into a nation of fussy, agitated, ornery and exasperated lunatics. It would threaten to kill our nation's economy because productivity would plummet due to all the man-hours needed to assault the Fortress.

JUNE 21, 2003

THE SURREALITIES OF THE SYSTEM

Below are some snippets that encompass some of our recent highs and lows…as well as some of the areas in between. If nothing else, navigating in the System has a habit of sending my delicate balance into convulsions. Please refrain from donating tongue suppressors; my foot will suffice as it far too frequently finds itself firmly inserted in my mouth.

MEDICAL

Kim's leg braces should be here in a few weeks. It is amazing how much stronger she is now. Our morning care provider left us so we've picked up most of the slack ourselves. Kim actually does way more than the care provider did! It's still very tiring work, but it shows just how much recovery of strength and stamina Kim has achieved. I am so proud of her. Her courage and determination are inspiring. I believe she will walk again and ask God for it daily.

I continue to hobble along, happy to have an intact foot. More important: just happy to be alive and together with my family. I've broken some rods and pins in my bionic foot and will need to get a parts upgrade in a few months. I'm expecting my new and improved version will be ready just in time to get a starring role in the next "Terminator" movie, which I am calling, "T4 – Wrong Turn at Roswell: Run For Your Lives: Return to the Mother Ship."

INSURANCE

The anecdotes about the absurdity of healthcare insurance are just too numerous to mention without turning this into a novelette or insane web-log (which, appropriately, is called a "blog," because it can "blog" you down and is capable of "blogging" your arteries). One worth mentioning was that, even before we left Denver, I received two separate lien notices from Kim's hospital placing claims against our house in San Francisco. The medical expenses were so great that the hospital worried that our insurance company would not provide reimbursement coverage. The liens totaled almost a million dollars, which was a lot of money back then. The hospital, therefore, put the pressure on me, figuring that I would be motivated to encourage payment from my insurer (to lean on them, so to speak) if our house were at risk.

Another, more recent case involves an invoice that I've submitted for reimbursement that keeps getting bounced back and forth between my insurer, the provider, and me because no one seems able to read. I have provided my insurer with all the information they've requested, but someone there keeps sending it back to me requesting the information I had just given them. It has gotten to be really funny because I keep the papers attached and simply add a new letter repeating the information and drawing an arrow to the previous recitation as well as the original mention of the "missing" information. The packet is getting quite large and will soon require more postage than the claim is actually worth. Clearly, the cost of man-hours expended on this bizarre paper chase has far exceeded either the cost to the insurer or the benefit to me. It is truly crazy...though, sadly, not uncommon. The realities of healthcare insurance are nothing if not surreal.

I always loved being awake and alive early in the morning. They were very enjoyable hours, and often remarkably productive. At the very least, I could be alone with my thoughts, if I had any, without subjecting them to the wants and needs of others. I could let my mind marinate in its own juices before daybreak when the rush hour emerged with a cascade of competing demands and agendas that ushered in an onslaught of new ingredients. After the accident, the darkness of the early morning also provided ample cover for my mind to roam about, in search of unexplored corners, crevices, or mud puddles in which to frolic. It often dragged along as playmates some of the troubling or unresolved issues that I may have been ignoring, either intentionally or, more likely inadvertently. Things piled up: some things got attention; others did not. Most things got way more attention than they deserved, but other things got way less than they needed. This is what the System ultimately conspired to achieve: an imbalance in our priorities.

CHAPTER FOURTEEN

SAFE AS MILK

*May cause nausea, cancer, internal bleeding, liver failure,
permanent blindness, or spontaneous combustion.*

AFTER WE PIERCED THE VEIL following our accident, your mother and I became part of a whole new world where prescription drugs were a necessary part of life. We didn't like the fact that we had to ingest mounds of pills and tablets, but we were living proof of just how beneficial certain medications could be. For example, the Vicodin–OxyContin cocktail I took for so many months did a wonderful job of masking the pain of my crushed foot. Unfortunately, this cocktail also deprived my brain of other sensations as well, including common sense and a modicum of rational thinking. I became kind of a zombie. I also became terribly addicted to Vicodin.

The problem I ran into was that I experienced tortuous withdrawal symptoms in the form of the most painful headaches you can imagine. Each one felt like an ice pick being slowly ground into the most sensitive part of my brain, before bending and trying to escape through one of my eye sockets. It was excruciating. I think if a gun had been close by I would have been tempted to use it. Of course, the only thing that would make the pain subside was, naturally, more

135

Vicodin. Great...so much for kicking the habit easily. Instead, I had to wean myself off the stuff over a period of several weeks.

The other interesting side effect of narcotics such as Vicodin was that they tended to make one constipated. This was not a trivial issue. I had been dutifully taking my prescribed painkillers for many days (perhaps a couple of weeks) when it dawned on me that I hadn't had a bowel movement in...God knew how long. I discreetly mentioned this to one of our more medically astute friends (i.e., a doctor) who told me not to worry about it.

"The doctors in Denver instructed you to use stool softeners, right?" he asked knowingly.

"No, they did not," I replied, growing a little nervous.

"Really?" he said, somewhat incredulously. "Well, they should have," he countered authoritatively, disapproving of a competitor's practice. "It's standard procedure."

"What should I do?" I asked, now getting worried.

"Well, for sure don't take a laxative," he commanded, now also looking a little concerned, "that would be a disaster."

"Well," I pressed on, "what should I do?"

"Take some stool softeners. You *should* have been taking them any way. But you might have to wait a while before they start to work."

"How long is 'a while'?" I asked, hopefully.

"Don't know," he replied uncertainly, "how many days has it been?"

"I can't remember."

"Well, then you've got a lot of stool to soften."

Great.

The strange thing about my foot that was crushed in the accident was that it was not terribly painful. Sure, it hurt a little, but the narcotics kept the discomfort at an acceptable level. Without question, the headaches from the Vicodin withdrawal were without compare. They were killers...or near suicide inducers. The next most painful experience, and perhaps the most disturbing, can be appropriately referred only to as "the Dump."

I cannot recall exactly when, but at some point after I started taking stool softeners, I realized that it was time to go. Not as in go *now*, but rather, fairly *soon*. Finally, the moment of truth arrived. It was, as I often liked to say, time to "talk to the President." This conversation, however, took a while, given that I had a lot "on my mind."

Without getting into too many details, the Dump turned into an event of epic proportions. Most impressive was not that I had a lot on my mind, but that it took me hours to say what I had to say. Furthermore, the pain of having so much to say, and of having to say it so sloooowly, caused me to emit horrific and unearthly sounds from the Presidential chamber.

Parents from faraway lands must have surely run to cover their children's ears. Wild dogs ran for cover. Alice Cooper and Ozzy Osbourne each came by and fought over my services as a back-up singer. My parents threatened to call in an Exorcist. The FBI thought they had located Osama Bin Laden. Nearby churches thought that the end times had arrived.

The conversation – the entire experience – was exhausting. The biggest lesson I can share with you, should you somehow be on a prescription of narcotics, is to always be sure to ask your doctor about stool softeners. *Please*.

Needless to say, despite your mother's incredible progress and recovery following the accident, the severity of her injuries resulted in numerous complications. Her physicians prescribed an arsenal of medications designed to counteract a myriad of maladies. It astounded me how many different types of drugs there were. I grew up thinking that aspirin was about the only medication one would ever need. Wrong. I began to realize how the pharmaceutical world could so effectively highlight the difference between what we thought we needed and what we ended up being prescribed.

Unfortunately, your mother really did require the majority of her medications. They helped control her pain and manage an assortment of other issues related specifically to her spinal cord injury. John Lennon was once quoted as saying, "Life without drugs would be impossible." At first, I thought he was simply playing his part as an icon of the 1960s hippie, counter-culture. I later learned, however, that his life as a professional musician was incredibly demanding and exhausting, even for a young man. The problem Lennon faced was that, while playing music could be exhilarating, the adrenaline created by playing was not conducive for going to sleep. Most musicians played live performances at night, which made sleeping at night a challenge. Friendly physicians, encouraged by band managers, were quick to hand the musical lad something to help him sleep.

But waking up on schedule and being productive during the day also proved to be a challenge because the young laddie went to bed so late at night. No worries, the friendly physician came along again, this time with a different pill to help give the lad a little spring in his step. Thus, the pattern was repeated until it became painfully obvious that these poor lads could neither go to bed nor wake up without the aid of drugs. John Lennon got in the habit of keeping his drugs in his refrigerator, where he would always be able to find them and where they would be, as he said, "Safe as milk."

JULY 17, 2003

DADDY'S DELIGHTS and DILEMMAS

I cannot prove it, but I'll wager anything that the makers of infant baby formula have somehow infused their mysterious product with Opium. Babies the world over crave it each day – can't live without it, in fact. No other single food item, person, or object creates the heightened sense of longing before its ingestion or state of bliss afterwards. In the process, these makers have created a cartel more powerful than enjoyed by any of the oil, auto, or diamond industries. In fact, I'm sure that those industries – indeed, ALL industries – are controlled by the makers of baby formula. Especially the popular media. Think about it: how else could we be trained to accept the spoon-feeding of daily doses of such inane drivel. Mmmmmm, so full of anti-flavor. More anti-flavor, please! And yet, as a new dad, I feel my role in this great conspiracy is firmly set. I am both at the mercy of my daughter's nutritional needs and a slave to the machine that is giving her such near-term bliss but ultimately leading her into the mouth of the Dragon of consumerism.

It was still early in the morning when Olivia started to give me that expectant look of anticipation. At her advanced age of nine months, she is now finely attuned to her specific likes and dislikes. What impresses me most is not so much her level of discernment but, rather, the unqualified certainty with which she approaches her judgment of things. We all have our morning rituals and requirements. Paramount for me, for example, is a robust cup of coffee (or two, or 20). This has been true for me ever since college, when I converted from being a night owl to an early riser. Now, of course, I am both.

Olivia's morning rituals consist of: (1) a hug from mom or dad, (2) a diaper change, and (3) a nice warm bottle of baby formula.

The first two warm my heart enormously. Olivia has always greeted us in the morning with a big smile and a big hug. Wouldn't it be great if we could all start the day with such a sunny disposition? The diaper change has also always been a pleasant experience (for Olivia, at least), for we have from day one used it as an opportunity to laugh, play, and, oddly, develop our vocabulary skills. Olivia's bottle desire, however, goes a bit beyond what I believe is a child's natural and simple need to satisfy hunger or oral stimulation.

Olivia is positively obsessed with her bottle. She seeks it out if it is not within her range of vision. Once she procures it, she prefers to take full control of its administering, grasping it firmly with both hands before then slipping into a more comfortable one-handed grip once a steady flow has been established. And then her trans-formation begins. Her head tilts back. Her eyes close. The features on her face soften (not an inconsequential feat for a chipmunk-cheeked baby). She settles into a trance...and she is gone. She is in another zone and on another planet for at least the next hour.

I thus made the brilliant but dangerous deduction that the magic ingredient in baby formula must be none else but the aforementioned and dreaded Opium. How else can one explain the hypnotic, trance-like effect this simple substance has on our sweet, innocent little child? She becomes completely content and totally unresponsive to all other stimuli. Knowing that she is now savagely addicted to this narcotic substance, I am almost powerless to change her behavior. I also feel like I am a conspirator in her ad-diction. I don't just escort her up to the dark, veiled door behind which lies the den of iniquity. No, I actually prepare the hookah, light the match, and give her the darned pipe.

In my bleary early morning state, I envision her wearing a silk robe and turban. I, on the other hand, am dressed like a nefarious, shadowy pusher, shepherding her into the den where liquid dreams commence upon procurement of the magic bottle. Eliciting dreams, doubtless, of shopping malls full of shoes, miniskirts, hair products, and very bad music. Soon to be followed by cars, jewelry, reality TV, and more bad music.

The dragon's mouth is large. The road to its gaping jaws starts, quite clearly, with Similac.

The prescription drug trade in America was big business. Like all of medicine, however, the pharmaceutical industry was been taken over by the insurance industry, which regulated prescription medications and determined who qualified for how much and when. For example, a physician would write a prescription for a specific medication to treat a specific condition. An unknown and unseen gatekeeper at an insurance company, however, would also determine that such a medication was too expensive and should, therefore, be substituted with a comparable alternative. Prescription switched. Or, more helpful, said gatekeeper would determine that the patient's condition did not warrant any medication at all. Prescription denied.

There were countless examples of this lunatic circus. Suppose a physician needed to change a prescription in order to alter its strength or dosage frequency. It sometimes took weeks for this change to be approved and effected. The pharmacist's hands were tied because she could not fill any prescription unless first approved by insurance. Such delays often prevented us from receiving medications when we needed them most. Naturally, such inconveniences occurred only with the most critical and important medications, never with the inconsequential ones.

I would get furious with these gatekeepers in the System who dictated and administered such practices. Did they have some outstanding medical competence? Had they been granted some sort of moral or voter mandate? Of course not. The only value they created was to further fill the pockets of those running the System. So, my rage against the System only intensified.

After your mother was released from her long stay in the Rehabilitation Unit at Valley Medical Center, I made weekly (and sometimes daily) visits to the local pharmacy to pick up her prescriptions. It was not something I particularly enjoyed doing, but it was an act of service that I felt compelled to do. It was a very small demonstration of my desire to care for and nurture my wife.

On one spectacularly beautiful, sunny California day, I was standing in line waiting to pick up a particularly large order of your mother's medications. When I got to the counter, the pharmacist started bringing out your mother's pills. They just kept coming and coming, more and more and more. I started sobbing right there in the pharmacy. *All these medications,* I thought. The experience hit home for me, in a profoundly new way, just how injured your mother really was. It made me so sad that she had to take so many pills just to try to combat her wounds and pains or treat her symptoms. None of these crazy pills would actually *cure* her; none of them would help her regain her legs. They were all designed – all of them – to help her get by and to cope with her new body. It made me incredibly sad.

Later that night, I went online and transferred all of our prescriptions to a mail-order fulfillment service. It was convenient and allowed me to avoid the self-inflicted emotional beatings incurred by having to physically retrieve your mother's medications from the pharmacy. I reasoned that, if picking up these medications caused me such angst and anguish, then I would, instead, let them come to me. Going out of my way to retrieve them literally added insult to injury.

Nevertheless, these powerful medications did indeed enable some elements of independence. But they also eroded another. Similarly, the mail-order service that processed and delivered the prescriptions provided some benefit, mostly convenience, but it came at the cost of making me further beholden to the System. There was no personal attention from a caring local pharmacist, prescription changes were expedited much slower than I had hoped (and needed), and we give up lots of quality control because we lost our personal physicians and local pharmacist as potential advocates because they were no longer involved in the delivery chain. They had been, according to a term common in my time, "disinter-mediated."

After we pierced the veil, I quickly noticed how all of us in my time had become prisoners of the System. We were addicted to medications (any substance, really) that made us feel good, and consequently we became beholden to the science that produced them and the services that dispensed them. Many years earlier, some federal agency mandated that the makers of cigarettes and hard alcohol could no longer advertise on television. Not long thereafter, pharmaceutical companies seized upon the opportunity to fill the airwaves with advertisements for more scientifically derived addictive products.

It became comical, really, how many advertisements for different prescription drugs we were subjected to. I swear, there were so many advertisements pitching the need to treat newly created maladies that I started to think that there were more disorders than there were orders. These slick adverts urged us to consult with our physician if we suffered from, say, "AINS – Active Itchy Navel Syndrome" to see if "Lint-Away" was right for us.

We were a nation hooked on drugs. We got pitched all these new drugs because they would enhance the quality of our lives. Perhaps. But they also created a belief that medications could treat all our woes. Ultimately, those magic pills could relieve everything…except consumerism. The Machine wanted us to be a nation of pill poppers because it was quick, easy, and guilt-free. It was also good for the economy and, not coincidentally, the pharmaceutical business.

The pharmaceutical industry was so profitable because, once people started taking a given medication, they might never stop taking it. If Big Pharma could get a child to start taking any kind of prescription at a young age, chances are they had a customer for life. The child would grow into someone who likely needed to take all kinds of medications that could assist in all the various stages of development. Of course, any associated side effects that arose from the prescribed medication could be easily treated…by another prescription. What a great business.

At some point in my time, we came to believe that all physical or emotional challenges were more like "flaws" that could be treated medically. Big Pharma had cleverly altered our thinking such that, as empowered consumers, we were justified to treat ourselves through modern medicine. It was a strange notion of entitlement based on a growing perception of easy elimination of life's imperfections through simple consumption of a pill or two. Companies were making a fortune selling us this junk. And, of course, many of these "enhancement" drugs were just as addictive as heroin, just less obvious. As any street corner dope peddler in my time said, "The first taste is always free; the others will cost you dearly."

The painful truth is that we medicated ourselves with far more than drugs. People in my world took anything to make themselves feel good. It was not the substances we were addicted to: it was pleasure. We would take anything, do anything, try anything to fill ourselves up with a sense of significance. We were always in search of some gratification, even if only a temporary high, that would ease the discontentment of our neglected inner selves, whom we feared to confront and confide in.

The only thing our inner selves really wanted was approval. More than simply satisfied, we desired to be accepted, embraced, and exalted.

In our quest, we filled ourselves up with everything under the sun. Yes, everything eventually wore off, disappointed or disappeared. Except for God's grace, which was free for us to accept at anytime. But the only way to accept *that* was through submission. Such a thought was more than most could bear, because it meant abandoning our attempts to seek fulfillment through our own efforts or consumptions.

We then tried to harbor the things we treasured, and tried to protect them so they would be "safe as milk." But we all knew that any milk, no matter how sweet, eventually turned sour.

CHAPTER FIFTEEN

JUSTICE

How far removed is too far away?

T HE LEGAL SYSTEM IN MY WORLD was a disaster. It confused justice with legality and vice versa. Basic moral fairness and justice were considered too simple for our evolved and sophisticated system of laws and amendments. The laws of man became more important than the laws of God. The legal system grew further removed from its original intent to help society function more fairly. Such became the injustice of justice: where the flower of a great endeavor was overrun by weeds that twisted intent and process to the point where perpetrators had more legal rights than their alleged victims.

AUGUST 20, 2003

AS TIME FLIES AND DRAGS

The last few weeks seemed to just race by. Time Flies. But time also is a drag. For example, the legal process just crawls along at its own glacial pace. "Due process," it's called. Can you believe that the fellow who hit us hasn't even been arraigned? I've mentioned before that our experience through this ordeal confirms my belief that the rights of the accused far outweigh those of the offended. I can appreciate mercy and extreme measures to avoid false accusation and punishment. But some cases are a little clearer than others. The problem is that the system has left no incentive to expedite anything. In fact, it's usually just the opposite: there is great incentive to delay and postpone and prolong. Meanwhile, the poor kid who hit us is hanging out waiting for a plea to some sentence that will be awful regardless of how much mercy the court extends him. And our family gets dragged along while we try to get our lives back in order.

It seems like Easter was just yesterday, and yet it was months ago. I love Easter because during that time of year, rebirth is everywhere all around us. Although Easter has come and gone, the good news is that we have the opportunity for ourselves to experience rebirth this very minute...and every subsequent minute. I need to remind myself of that, especially late at night or early in the morning when I am dragging and dreary. Anyway, part of experiencing rebirth is to be mindful and appreciative of all the gifts around us.

It is just insane how much we have to be thankful for. Imagine if we'd had our accident in Iraq. Good grief, we'd have no chance at a normal life afterwards. Imagine if we lived in Iraq. Imagine if we lived in America...1000 years ago. Imagine if we were sea turtles...on land. Imagine if we had, like millions of people today, no reason to have much hope about anything. That, my friends, is both sad and quite terrifying.

Thankfully, Olivia continues to be a wonderful baby. What a joy. What a blessing. What a sight to see how much she loves her mother. What a delight to know that time with her just flies by. What a drag that we can't slow it down and savor such moments.

DECISIONS, DECISIONS

There are some things in life about which we have no choice. For example, our skin color, the number of digits we are born with, and how tall or short we eventually become. We have no control over their outcome. There are other things, however, for which we have many choices and where our input can have a great influence on the final outcome.

In America, it was astonishing to consider how many decisions were required of us in any given day. Our multitude of options was derived from our productive, abundant resources and driven by enterprising individuals who benefitted from the vision of our founding fathers, who believed that people need not be bound by their birth status or the occupations of their ancestors. Unshackled enterprise thus created a plethora of consumer choices that broadened individual preferences but could cripple one's mind when calculating the available options. For example, just choosing which wine varietal best complemented a particular meal was almost as vexing as the dilemma of which salad dressing best accompanied a certain strain of lettuce. It took most people more time to decide upon and purchase a pair of shoes than to buy a car or house.

More significant, of course, were the decisions about how we chose to live, how we reacted to circumstances, and how we chose to perceive the events in our lives. Playing armchair coach during the Super Bowl was pretty easy, but how we chose to treat others who had wronged us was quite a bit thornier.

An unsavory aftermath of the accident required our involvement in the legal system. As part of that ugly process, we were asked by the Boulder County District Attorney to express our thoughts on the punishment that the young man who hit us should receive. The DA and presiding judge had a wide variety of options at their disposal.

These options ranged from a long prison term to probation to restitution to community service, and any combination thereof.

At face value, it seemed easy: a crime was committed, people have suffered and proper punishment should result. No measure, of punishment, of course, could return us to our condition before our accident on October 12.

It was among the most challenging dilemmas I had ever confronted. To be sure, it was our great hope that this young man could somehow serve as an example to help others from committing a similar mistake in the future. How that was ultimately achieved, of course, would be determined by how he chose to perceive both his actions and the resulting consequences. We had no interest in revenge, but we did desire justice through a sentence that attempted to balance punishment and mercy.

As I contemplated this delicate ratio in a manner consistent with how I thought Jesus would respond, I confronted the parallels in the judgment of my own life, and how I chose to live it. All of my decisions and choices became glaringly exposed. The light of truth on my own sins and transgressions revealed the simple reality that we were usually not the best judges of our own lives and how we affected others. We were too partial and, for obvious reasons, self-righteous. Thankfully, there were judges who handled criminal cases and another judge, God, who handled everything else.

JULY 29, 2003

THERMOSTAT & ATTITUDE ADJUSTMENT

We can't control what happens to us, but we can control how we respond. That response is what makes up character and integrity. As well as central air conditioning.

The weather over the last few days has been stiflingly hot, often to point of steaming, which is ironic because our heat here is dry, not humid. Therefore, I've reasoned that the steam I see must be that which comes out of my ears every time I contemplate either our legal and insurance hassles. It's nice to be able to generate one's own microclimate. My internal thermostat is located somewhere between my heart and soul with a wireless connection placed somewhere in my mind – lost amidst the piles of priorities and stacks of concerns I've collected but have yet to fully dispel or shred.

Proper climate control, however, requires a discipline and wisdom I'll never have. The Buddha had those qualities as does the Dalai Lama. Jesus also had the ability to control his internal weather pattern, though he didn't hide from his emotions or minimize them.

As I've said before, a mind is a terrible thing, especially when it conjures up spontaneous, nasty thoughts without my approval. I need to hire an assistant for my mind who will screen such spontaneous neurotic "mind-mails" and prevent them from reaching the already cluttered desktop of my consciousness. (Note to self: Good luck.)

A newspaper in Denver covered the story of Mr. Zachery's sentencing. Our accident had touched a number of lives in the local community, especially the high school, where Mr. Zachery and his best friend attended. The story was sympathetic and emotional, and it emphasized how Mr. Zachery's life would never be the same. The account, however, hit a raw nerve with me because it practically argued Mr. Zachery's innocence in its desperate attempt to convey extenuating circumstances and ulterior motives. Like the legal system, the article seemed more sympathetic to the perpetrator than the victims.

In the world of my time, the media had an incessant desire to practice perfect political correctness in the hopes of achieving some higher state of Zen-like inner peace. The media's version of political correctness was that there were at least two sides to every story, each deserving of equal time, respect, and moral consideration. The media seemed to apply this standard even to cases like our accident, where there was really no need to have two "sides" to the story. In life, some events were good and some were bad. Why or even how they happened might have been interesting or compelling, but they should not have taken precedence over the simple facts surrounding the incident itself.

AUGUST 5, 2003

LIBERTY AND JUSTICE FOR ALL

I just learned that Joseph Zachery, the young man who plowed into us, was sentenced last Friday. The judge's decision is somewhat frustrating. I am being a bit "diplomatic" here. I actually found it outrageously insulting. The presiding judge sentenced Zachery to 90 days in county jail and six years of 'community corrections," which is essentially a half way house program.

Obviously, the judge did not share our beliefs and did not send the kind of message we were hoping for. I think he missed a real opportunity to send a powerful message and make a meaningful impact. What a pity to compound a tragedy with this kind of judicial response. Or, rather, lack of response.

Again, because the damage to us cannot be undone, I don't have any personal interest in whether Zachery goes to jail for one day or a hundred years. I am very passionate, however, that his punishment should serve as a lesson and a deterrent for others tempted to commit similar crimes. I hope the judge cares enough about the youth of his community to send a wise message of tough love to those who wreck people's lives. Otherwise, it will be an enormous insult to us and all the other victims of such blatantly reckless and dangerous behavior.

Please don't think that I vilified Mr. Zachery. I certainly did not condone his actions or behavior, but I also recognized that he, too, was deserving of our prayers. He was a very young man whose life would likely be filled with torment and anguish. I remember when I was his age – though I really don't want to.

My teenage years were a terrible time. I was growing like a weed, strong as an ox, and felt almost invincible, at least physically. I was full of testosterone, yet socially inept, loaded with energy, yet had zero self-confidence. I was not really a bad kid, but I was susceptible to those who may have been. In other words, I was a typical teenage male in America. And I had all kinds of advantages going for me: good parents and stable family, small town values, good education, heavy involvement in sports, and strong involvement in my church.

My understanding was that Mr. Zachery was not as fortunate in some respects. I knew, for example, that his parents had been recently divorced. Like many teenage boys, he acted out his anger, frustration, confusion, and abandonment behind the wheel of a car that, in such a state, was a lethal weapon.

I now think that the only way to diffuse such WMDs (Weapons of Mass Destruction) is through the combination of awareness, understanding, and communication. Kids may not always have the best venue at home for such a process. School can help, and church can really help. Your mother and I often thought that schools should teach situational case studies that involved assessment, evaluation, and discussion with other kids. We thought the process would foster responsible decisions out in the real world.

In such an ideal world, I would have loved being a teacher. Nevertheless, I am sure I would have been a fantastical failure. My two main strengths – idealism and long-winded discourses – would have surely created a room full of slumbering students. The media, of course, would have quickly learned of the scandalous snore-fest and jumped to exploit such a disgraceful waste of potential learning on their youth. Unfortunately for the kids, the media would have botched its coverage of the classroom siestas. It would have wanted to cover both "sides" of the event in order to get the full story. I would have naturally talked about how bad I felt, and how the system had failed me, and all that; but the truth was I had bored the students senseless. The kids, justifiably, would have been speechless.

SEPTEMBER 12, 2003

WE READ THE NEWS TODAY...OH LORD

Yesterday morning I received an email from the Boulder District Attorney stating that Joseph Zachery, the young man whose car hit us head-on, had walked away from his halfway house and was, therefore, considered an escapee. The DA shortly followed up with message that Mr. Zachery had been found but had tragically committed suicide by hanging himself.

Such terrible news. That was certainly the last thing we wanted for him. What makes us really sad for Joseph is that it seemed to us that he was crying out for help for a long time and no one seemed to hear or care. Surely there were signs that teachers or concerned observers might have noticed. Most recently, the entire legal system let him down. His charges were practically dismissed by the court, giving Joseph another out and another false indication that actions don't carry consequences. He even said in his court testimony that he wanted to be punished for his actions...his soul knew.

Joseph's suicide was yet another heartbreaking punctuation on a long-running saga. For those of us who had to carry on, his suicide left a sad and indelible earmark on a chapter already full of sadness. We barely saw Mr. Zachery's car when it hit us that night and there was certainly nothing we could have done to prevent that collision. His dreadful ending, however, was something that someone should have seen coming from miles away.

How sad. How very sad.

CHAPTER SIXTEEN

LETTING IN AND LETTING GO

Not even sponges are born with infinite absorption capacity.

WHILE YOUR MOTHER WAS IN REHABILITATION, life for us seemed like it was on hold. It was suspended in a state of uncertainty, powered by prayers that God would grant her a miraculous recovery, and prolonged by our holding out for the possibility that this was all just a bad dream...that it had never actually happened. These weeks and months were spent within a cloud of fog. We were part of the world, but mostly detached from it, coolly disconnected from the world we were hovering over, hoping that a warm wind would send us back into the ocean from which we came. And so, like a San Francisco summer fog, we kept hovering, lingering...and waiting.

The fog eventually lifted when your mother finally escaped rehab and came to live with us at the Compound in Cupertino. We began to see more clearly that our new reality was what we had been hoping we could avoid: that we had indeed been awake and that our state of being was here to stay. Life was beginning anew. A little different and a little scary, but at least we were all together, intact and determined to make the best of it.

The first order of business was to for you to reestablish a bond with your mother. This had been her most pressing concern from the moment she regained awareness after the accident. Your mother obsessed constantly over this issue: How would this affect Olivia, having a mother who is incapacitated and unable to establish that important bond during early childhood? Her concern about your early development is why we brought you to the hospital every day, so that the two of you could connect, as best you could, even within the not-so-cuddly confines of a hospital bed.

After your mother was home with us, we were finally able to help nurture that connection. You and she had to fully let each other in, something that was compromised because of the accident and the hospital beds. Only after the fog lifted, with all of our defenses dissipated, could all of us – not just you and your mother – embrace that process.

We learned that, in order to truly let something in, we had to first let something go. The act of releasing, of opening up by letting go, created the wherewithal – the physical, emotional, or spiritual space – that was required to receive freely and without reservation.

I quickly realized that letting in was relatively easy; letting go was an altogether different matter. Letting go of some things was as natural as dropping a hot potato or flushing the toilet. For example, I needed to let go of some obvious baggage, such as certain physical expectations, a distant goal or two, and the stubborn defenses of denial that I had erected in the desperate hope of not having to let in a new reality. On the other hand, certain other things, proved much more challenging to let go of.

The first was Duffy, our beloved Scottish terrier. In truth, Duffy had been getting old, and he was showing signs of weakness long before the accident. Your mother and I had even sensed that Duffy was hanging around just long enough to welcome you into the world before departing it himself.

By the time we had relocated to the Compound after the accident, Duffy's spark had diminished further, and he was on his last legs. We sometimes brought him to the hospital so your mother could see him, which brightened both of them immeasurably. But back home, Duffy was quickly dying. I am certain that he was also mourning your mother.

When your mother finally came home for good, she faced the harsh reality that Duffy was beginning to suffer. It took her longer than the rest of us to accept it. She had lost so much so quickly; she couldn't bear to now lose her dog of 15 years. Your mother and I had long joked that Duffy had been great training in preparing us for children. He certainly was, and he successfully completed that mission.

Letting go of Duffy was among the hardest, most heart-breaking things we ever went through. Not because he was a beloved pet, but because of what letting go of him represented in the whole scheme of things that made up our upside-down world. So much loss, so much suffering, so many things being taken away.

Nevertheless, letting go of Duffy meant that you and your mother could fully connect and bond. Duffy's absence propelled the two of you together in a way that might have been more difficult, or taken longer, had he lingered longer. Painful as it was to go through, the end result was a blessing far greater than any we could have ever derived from merely clinging – fearfully and desperately – to that which we knew deserved to be let go.

The other big piece of baggage that I needed to let go of was my stiff upper lip and my stalwart defenses of determination to appear like I had everything under control and was keeping it all together.

Even if I did not, I presumed that sheer will-power could alter my ability to cope.

In public, the notion of "fake it till you make it" was admirable and occasionally effective. I began to realize, however, that in God's eyes, such a notion didn't fly. He didn't expect me to fake it; he expected me to be authentic and transparent.

My strength alone was not sufficient; it could not sustain us. Only by relinquishing my own inadequate strength – by letting go of it – could I fully embrace my own weakness and therefore allow God's strength to accomplish everything that I could not. To execute His plan, not mine.

I realized that I needed to not just decide that I needed God in my life, but that I needed to yield to Him. I needed to let God in and take over. The only way I could do so was to give up that which was preventing me from being truly broken. I needed to let go of the blanket of strength that I had woven so poorly that it was barely concealing my inadequacies. I needed to let go and relinquish my pride that had so weakly supported the nobility of my disposition. The steel of my pride did not have adequate tensile strength to bear the load that I was asking it to carry. Only God's grace was capable of removing that load completely from my weakness and transferring it to His strength.

SEPTEMBER 27, 2003

A HOUSE AT LAST

After months of searching, we finally bought a house that would work for us. I saw this house on Friday afternoon, brought Kim over to see it on Saturday and made our offer on Sunday. The crazy thing is that I've spent more time deliberating over a pair of shoes than I spent on this house.

I used to think when I was a kid that if I ever owned a house this expensive that I would be, by definition, rich. Well, kid, times change. While I am not exactly house-poor, I'm certainly not exactly. Of course, I would be if I lived in some far-flung, "lesser developed" corner of the world.

Even the poorest of Americans would be "rich" if we lived amongst the poorest of the world's "poor." I'm not sure our "rich-ness" is any more valuable than their "poor-ness." In fact, I think "lesser-developed" simply refers to countries where the systems of separating people from their money are not yet fully established or operationally efficient.

Nevertheless, the world is built around efforts to accumulate that which is most valuable to a particular person or society. Everything is fine until those things are removed or taken away. What then, do we do? How do we react? This is the struggle that defines the human condition. We want something, and God usually provides it. And then it goes away or is taken from us. So we ask ourselves: "Was that what I really wanted? What do I do now? Where do I find my strength and comfort if what used to give me comfort is no longer available? On whom or what can I lean for support and encouragement? Where should I focus my thoughts and attention? What should I do with my time? With my life?

Will we turn to God when we are stripped of what matters most to us? Or will we be bitter, angry, vengeful, or despairing? If our goal is to get those things back, will our sights be on anything else other than God to help us attain them? And, the deeper question is whether our goal should be anything other than getting closer to God. Were we stripped of our prized possession principally for the sake of allowing us a new opportunity to choose between it and God? Should we not prize God first? If so, then all those things we thought were so valuable are considerably less so.

The problem is that we almost always choose something else over God. That, in my opinion, is the true nature of the human condition; it is our singular struggle. Individual challenges, like the kind resulting from our accident, often reveal what we most value and cherish because they will be exposed and tested in ways that we never could have imagined. In my case, I've come to realize that the thing I've worshipped more highly than others is my sense of control and autonomy.

Returning to the comparatively less threatening topic of Bay Area real estate, I am not sure that a house purchase in California is a great investment at present. The economy here has some major structural challenges, namely, a high-cost business environment and a new found trend for the faster growing sectors to outsource skilled jobs overseas. It is definitely a changing landscape. Additionally, I believe we have simply traded one asset bubble (technology stocks) for another (real estate). This has been exacerbated by very liberal interest rates designed to promote business spending and investment. The big Internet bubble may have popped, but there are still many smaller ones that sprouted because of it. They may be submerged under water, but they are growing in size as they float to the surface.

Nevertheless, despite my bearish outlook I am excited and relieved that we can finally settle into a place of our own and get on with the next phase of our lives. It has been very difficult to be in a state of transition for so long. We are very grateful for the house (the "Compound") we have been renting here in Cupertino, but it has been very trying because so much of it is inaccessible to Kim. This house was supposed to be a transitional outpost, and I never dreamed that we would be here so many months. We needed to be on more stable ground, though I'm not sure there really is such a thing, especially in California.

It was time to get resettled…again. The movers delivered a huge truckload of our belongings to the new house. We had never bothered to have those items delivered to our temporary residence in Cupertino because we had no idea how long we would be staying there.

Our belongings descended upon us like a snowstorm in July as we were completely unprepared for such a barrage. I thought, what the hell is all that stuff? We had lived such a Spartan lifestyle in Cupertino that the re-emergence of our stuff – much of it forgotten – took our breath away. There was so much. Our garage quickly filled with boxes that Kim and I had never packed. The Care Team had done an incredible job of packing up our old house. Perhaps they did too good a job. They packed everything. I would probably have discarded much of it, but because your mother and I weren't available to help provide guidance in the process, everything was saved and stored. Even little paper scraps. It took months to sort through everything and determine what was worth keeping and then deciding where on earth to put it.

Thus began yet another opportunity to test our skills of letting in and letting go. Less of the stuff and more of the meanings and memories attached. Even if I had been able to ditch everything and leave it all behind, the meaning that those things had for me – that I stayed attached to – would have made passing through the proverbial eye of the needle impossibly difficult. I would have been "stuck" – first by the needle and then in it.

OCTOBER 1, 2003

IN YOUR EYES

A recent cross-country flight allowed me a rare opportunity to pray, reflect and contemplate. As much as I often like to say that we have to move forward (and not look back), the truth is that I haven't had much time to process all that has transpired during the past half year. Even more truthful is that I don't really like to give myself time to process, because it is painful. Furthermore, I would rather put my energies toward making the most of the present and, if possible, helping to actualize a more positive future.

Nevertheless, six hours on a plane is a long time, and as I've said before, a mind can be a terrible thing. It is certainly sneaky. But it is always truthful. Not surprisingly, I reflected on some of the issues that sometimes keep me in my bunker of melancholy:

- Kim's nerve pain, which we don't often discuss with others.
- Our exhaustion, which is almost constant.
- The drain on our resources and energies.
- The amazing amount of time, money, and energy that we have expended solely as a result of the accident.

The collision of these thoughts and emotions, perhaps accentuated at 36,000 feet, brought to mind verses from one of our favorite songs:

> *I don't like to see so much pain,*
> *So much wasted...*
> *And each moment is slipping away.*
> *I get so tired...*
> *Working so hard for our survival.*
> *But I look to these times with you*
> *To keep me awake and alive.*
> *(Peter Gabriel – "In Your Eyes")*

Despite my somber reflections, three absolute joyful blessings stand out in stunning clarity. Amazingly, without the accident, these three things would have, potentially, simply been a part of our life's landscape instead of the reconstructed foundational bedrock we're rebuilding our lives on. They are, simply:

1) God's personal and merciful presence in our lives, which gives us, like King David, sustaining assurance to be courageous;

2) Olivia, our miraculous daughter, who has defied logic in every way; and

3) Family and friends, whose utterly amazing and humbling love and support we feel wholly undeserving. Sadly, it is something that we are ill equipped to ever properly acknowledge or repay.

Moving into our new house was a momentous event for us. I wish I could say that we felt a sense of excitement. In truth, it was more a sense of relief. We had been in a state of suspended animation for a long time, not knowing how much your mother might recover from her injuries, what our general needs would look like, and, accordingly, where we might relocate. In the 13 months preceding our move, your mother had been forced to bounce around so much that it practically caused motion sickness. She spent one week at a hospital in San Francisco after your birth, two weeks back at our house, then one night at a hotel in Denver before the accident, three weeks at a hospital in Denver, an extended stay of three months at a hospital in San Jose; and then another extended stay of eight months at a rental house in Cupertino. Your mother spent every one of those nights in recovery and, sadly, in incredible discomfort.

It was finally time to let go of our suspended state of uncertainty and allow ourselves to drop down to who knew where. We had to let go physically and emotionally in order to leave behind a life that was no longer available to us. The only way for us to create a new life was to let go of our old one.

CHAPTER SEVENTEEN

LURKING WITHIN

A buried emotion never dies.

*E*VENTUALLY, WE STARTED TO FEEL THAT LIFE was beginning to get back on track. We were adjusting to our new normal and starting to get comfortable with our new routines. But, just when we thought the Dragon had left us or moved out of our lives, something always happened that pulled us back into its ferocious clutches. It was always there, just waiting…lurking just beneath the surface.

In God's world, everything had a purpose…even my perceived temporary, terrestrial discomfort. The Greek playwright Aeschylus expressed it beautifully:

He who learns must suffer

And even in our sleep pain that cannot forget

Falls drop by drop upon the heart,

And in our own despair, against our will,

Comes wisdom to us by the awful grace of God.

(Agamemnon)

God's grace is wonderful because He gives it unconditionally. But it is awful because I knew that in order for me to receive it fully, certain parts of me needed to die, or at least be broken. What needed to be broken most of all was my pride.

The Dragon, my Tormentor, fed on the harshness of my life and encouraged me to engage in hurtful behavior, especially toward those I loved most. The harshness of my life, however, was my own creation. It came from my own sense of pride and self-centeredness.

The accident shattered our world. But I was shaken to my core when I realized that the Dragon – my Tormentor – did not simply emerge out of the blue in the arbitrariness of the accident. No, in fact, much to my horror and disgust, the Dragon was part of my own prideful and sinful nature, which had lived within me long before our near-fatal collision. Perhaps it took the horrors of the accident for the Dragon to emerge enough for me to see it, but it had always dwelt within me, lurking and actively nurturing all the contemptible thoughts and behaviors that I engaged in, but which I denied or refused to acknowledge.

Unlike a piece of shrapnel from a bomb born of malicious intent, the Dragon did not affix itself to me in the accident. The Dragon did not thrust itself on me through the accident, but it became a convenient excuse for me to claim that my Tormentor was a new and unwanted visitor, born of tragedy and designed to perpetuate misery. That pain was magnified when I realized that my Tormentor was really a creature of my own making. One that served to light the fire of my own selfish interests, which then unintentionally distanced me from God and my loved ones.

I was able to assist your mother in certain areas with a very loving heart and a sincere desire to care for her. But to some extent, I bent over backwards to help her – often to the point where she didn't need it or want it. My intentions became misaligned because I inadvertently disempowered her. My over-protectiveness inhibited her need for growth and independence. Even if she fell, made mistakes, or encountered awkward entanglements, your mother needed to experience them. But I had been preventing them, wanting to protect her from those "burdens" by taking them on myself. My Tormentor made it easy – almost acceptable – to feel that my actions deserved some kind of self-martyred sanctification.

My Tormentor was at its strongest – and became revitalized – during those times when my pride allowed me to think that I had defeated it. That I had somehow actually subdued my Tormentor and rendered it impotent solely through my own inner strength and determination. Nevertheless, despite my Tormentor's menacing intent, it served me well by its re-emergence during such times. It made me understand – ever more fully – that my isolated efforts were wholly ineffective against such an adversary. It made me realize that it was God's grace alone that spared me from complete torment and destruction.

I was determined to not allow my Tormentor to inhabit my life and inhibit my enthusiasm. Unfortunately, I lived under the false self-delusion that I was constantly connected to God. Despite my practical assumptions that it would have been easier and more efficient if I were to stay connected, my Tormentor helped me realize, however, that for me, being reconnected needed to happen every day, all the time…not just once.

So, in a strange way, I thanked my Tormentor for helping me – forcing me – to lean more fully on God. It forced me to choose one of only three paths:

1) Engage my Tormentor in battle…and lose;

2) Surrender myself to my Tormentor…and lose;

3) Surrender myself to God…and let God determine the outcome.

I learned that a buried emotion never dies. The only way to properly eradicate it is to exhume it and expose it to natural light, much the way one kills a vampire. Buried emotions are always waiting spring to life.

For example, just when I thought I'd gotten past the emotional trauma of the accident, I received a letter in the mail that contained a newspaper article about a Denver-area high school that had re-enacted our accident as part of a drunk driving awareness program. The article was noteworthy for me because it included a photograph of a young girl who was playing the role of your mother. The photo took my breath away. She had long, red hair, like your mother, and her face, covered in pretend blood, was captured in a moment of screaming agony. Your mother must have suffered incredibly.

This depiction of your mother made me shudder and just broke my heart. The image brought back for me all the memories of the accident that I had been able to suppress. I hadn't been able to really see your mother as I was trapped in the front seat. And I had not been able to comfort her. It made me feel so weak and helpless. I could feel that familiar pit stirring in my stomach.

Thankfully, your mother had no recollection of the accident or the agony she endured. I thanked God for that, because she didn't need to relive it again. I, on the other hand, could not forget it. Although I never experienced the flashbacks that people warned me about, the photograph in the newspaper brought it all back to life more insidiously than a buried emotion. The photograph provided a picture of your mother in her distress that my mind had not previously created or retained. The photo gave more color than I wanted or needed but also enabled me to confront head-on the horror and anguish that I'd been suppressing.

IRREGULAR, UNSCHEDULED MAINTENANCE

I endured in the daily grind of life, driving hard and fast, as if in a race of undermined length with unusual obstacles. I felt I needed – or at least allowed myself – occasional self-indulgent pit stops for refueling and tune-ups. The parts in my garage included God, cigars, wine, and donuts.

GOD

In my world, many secularists mocked faith or religion because they viewed it as a crutch, something that was needed only by those who were weak. Those who were strong, they argued, were more mentally and emotionally secure and, therefore, did not need faith or religion to help them get through life. As a young man, long before our accident, I was afraid or embarrassed to admit my weaknesses. Afterwards, when I was more seasoned and a lot less concerned with how I was generally perceived, I freely admitted that, for me at least, God was the only crutch that gave me true strength.

We all had crutches of some form or another. Some of us preferred money, fast cars, clothing, food, booze, power…whatever. The more I leaned on those kind crutches, however, the weaker I became. Conversely, the more I leaned on God, the stronger I became. I gained His strength through my weakness.

My problem was that, when I felt strengthened, I was sometimes prone to thinking that it was my doing and not His. I felt proud that my strength was self-imposed, rather than feeling blessed that it was God who had actually strengthened me.

Ironically, therefore, God wanted me broken because that was truly the only way I could connect with Him at the time. I did not want to be broken. But as I learned to better recognize the extent to which I already was, I learned to present my brokenness to Him more fully and honestly. Of course, there were those times I was unwilling to acknowledge my brokenness. Those were the times when I was most vulnerable and my Tormentor encouraged me to be strong, self-determined, and master of my universe. My Tormentor prevailed when I started to ask God to serve me instead of asking God how I could serve Him.

When my Tormentor got me in such a place, I was easy prey for my other favorite crutches, to all of which I felt I was entitled. They gave me pleasure, which I believe God found okay, within reason. Unless, of course, I enjoyed these things to excess, transforming them into implements of my own destruction.

CIGARS

Your great-great-grandfather was a tobacco grower in Connecticut. He made excellent cigars that won gold medals in Europe and, doubtless, were enjoyed by many of the captains of industry of his time. I was not raised as a cigar smoker, but I later became captivated by the allure of what cigars represented. Money, power, independence, and, above all, a certain element of male bonding that became uniquely cultivated over a good cigar.

Long before the accident, I eagerly anticipated the rare occasions when I happened to be on the East Coast and could spend the evening with a group of friends from the New Canaan Society, bonding over cigars into the wee hours of the night. My dear friend Jim was easily classified as a captain of industry. He hosted these little soirees at his southern Connecticut home, and he embodied the prototypical image of what a good cigar man should be: successful, handsome, a good family man, a pillar of his community, and fully alive for God. Therefore, every time I lit up a cigar, I thought of Jim...and God.

The thing I loved about cigars is that they forced me to relax. It was very difficult to remain stressed out after I had been smoking a cigar for a few minutes. Furthermore, cigars helped me connect to God. There was something spiritual about cigars. They came from the earth, and they helped me to slow down and get grounded, as if pulling me down to the earth from which they themselves emerged.

After the accident, I found special solace in cigars. Our new situation gave me considerable stress because I felt I was juggling so many balls and doing so many things to keep it together and re-build our lives. Cigars became more than my refuge; they became my escape.

WINE

I found it difficult to imagine a good cigar without a good glass of wine. Or whatever name-your beverage-of-choice. After the accident, I stayed clear of alcohol due to all the narcotics I was taking. After I completed my withdrawal from Vicodin, however, a glass of wine became, again, a nice complement to the evening meal. Well, you can already anticipate the slippery slope. Before I knew it, my stress level during the day warranted a glass of wine before dinner to help me relax. Another glass or two with dinner, then another afterwards with a cigar. Soon it started to get ugly. Mind you, it was very easy for me to feel justified in drinking a few glasses of wine. And there were times when it was indeed all right…just not all the time.

What I eventually realized, however, was that instead of helping me to relax and become reconnected with what mattered most in my life – God, my family, and friends – wine served to further discon-nect me from them. It served to help me sink further into my inner chamber instead of opening up and letting the world in. Wine did not become a problem, but it did become a crutch…the kind I didn't want to advertise on my sleeve. My Tormentor, of course, loved this because it loved every crutch other than God.

DONUTS

I loved donuts. I developed my first appreciation for them after early morning hockey practices when I was an impressionable pre-teenager. My father or mother dutifully awoke at pre-dawn hours in order to drive me to the sport I loved. After practices, we'd stop by a coffee shop where I quickly learned that donuts were gloriously delicious. At first, especially as a kid, they seemed relatively harmless. But, oh, the dangers that lurked down the road.

Like heroin, the first taste was always free. However, unlike dope peddlers who had to hide on shadowy street corners, donut pushers could operate in clean, well-lighted places and hand out free samples in full view of approving, on-looking parents. That first taste was deliriously intoxicating.

In hindsight, it was like some forbidden manna, but when I was a kid, it was better than candy for breakfast. Also, looking back, I think all the adults present were part of a secret society of donut addicts and silently conspired to introduce others into their quirky cult. It felt like a scene from "Invasion of the Body Snatchers," in which, after tasting the forbidden fruit, the gathered clan of adults exclaimed to each other telepathically: "Hooray! He's one of us now."

Thus began my long affair with the risen dough. It started off innocently enough as a kid, with occasional special treats after hockey games or practices. Indeed, the very scarcity of those special occasions made my longing and desire for those sweet rings of heaven all the more pronounced. It made me a slave to those seductively sweet, deep-fried beauties.

For many years, my cravings were hardly dangerous. There was always an adequate supply of donuts, and I never worried much about over-indulgence: my body type, metabolism, and rate of physical activity quickly worked off any of the potential side effects from occasional excessive indulgences. Eventually, of course, the onset of years changed all that. I think it was essentially parenthood, which conveniently coincided with the onset of middle-aged bloat, and my corresponding diminished ability to participate in any physical activity that involved anything more demanding than, say, breathing.

MEMORY LANE

About two years after the accident, I had to travel back to Denver for business. I underestimated the trepidation I would feel by being back in Denver, the scene of our accident, and, worse still, driving in the area.

Oh well. I put on my stiff upper lip and hoped for the best, looking forward to a little time in nature once outside the greater Denver area. I was completely unprepared for where my journey would take me. I was dutifully following my directions when, only a few minutes into my drive, I got a growing sense of dread. The highway started to look familiar. Then I saw a road sign indicating a town I recognized.

Suddenly, beyond my wildest expectations, I saw the very hotel in which we had woken up the day of the accident. I couldn't believe it. And then, as if my Tormentor had recruited Satan himself to write this diabolical drama, the exit ramp for the very road on which our accident occurred loomed just on the horizon. It was as if my eyes transformed themselves into a telescope and zoomed in solely on that exit, ignoring everything else in view.

It all came flooding back to me. Everything. Leaving the wedding, getting into our car, the eyes of the Dragon, the eyes of a boy about to die, your crying, your mother's moaning, tasting blood, feeling trapped, feeling helpless….the ambulance ride, the emergency room, the smell of ammonia that was used to wake me up. The dread of waking up and knowing what had happened. The police asking me to relive every last detail of the accident. The ambulance ride to be with your mother in her hospital. The smell of antiseptic everywhere. The squeaking sound that my wheelchair made on the ultra-clean floors. The "SICU" sign over the doorway of your mother's hospital ward, designating the place reserved for the very sick or injured. The strains of living at Yaffe House, of having to give myself blood thinner injections but unable to even change your diapers. Feeling helpless, feeling afraid, and feeling like I had done so little, feeling like I was still trying to figure out what I could do.

My eyes filled with tears and I could barely see, but I had to keep going. I had to put some distance between myself and this horrible place. I had to keep driving. I finally cleared my eyes and called your Aunt Margot from my cell phone. I had to talk with someone, and I couldn't call your mother. I just couldn't immerse her back into this morass, back to the place of her near death, to a place she didn't even remember.

Your Aunt Margot helped me get through it with her unique ability to get me laughing within minutes. Laughter was such good therapy. I think it should be prescribed for everyone who takes themselves too seriously. And for those who felt that their Tormentor was just a little too close at hand.

CHAPTER EIGHTEEN

RE-ENGAGEMENT

Being easily amused is not as bad as it's cracked up to be.

*I*N THE BLINK OF AN EYE, OUR WORLD and what we thought were dreams had been shattered. We prayed that we would be able to return to a place where we could dream again, if only to replace the nightmare that had invaded our lives. To do so, however, entailed a huge challenge that, if taken, required an active, deliberate decision to try to put ourselves in a place where we could be more thankful, more grateful, and more aware of the sheer gift of our survival, and less angry and fearful of what survival in our new state would entail.

After feeling somewhat powerless for so long, it was hard to take back control. It had to be done gradually...and with some care and thoughtfulness. Ideally, we should have employed some kind of strategic plan, but we didn't. With the benefit of hindsight, it's easy for me now to see how beneficial one would have been. But, as things were back then, we had our hands full just trying to get through each day. Re-engaging meant confronting unique fears and challenges but also realizing a great opportunity. And taking bold action.

OCTOBER 5, 2003

WITH OR WITHOUT

There are emotionally heart-wrenching highs and lows after a paralyzing injury such as Kim's. People who suffer from similar injuries or illnesses fall quickly into two camps: those who are angry and bitter and remain resentful of their situation (like I probably sound, ranting about the System and the Machine!), and those who are grateful to be alive and optimistic that they can successfully rebuild their lives. The accidents that often cause these injuries are usually quite horrific, as was ours. Interestingly, very few of these accident victims who are so seriously injured remember their accidents. Most are completely void of any memory of events a few hours before and several days (if not weeks) afterwards.

Why then am I confident and hopeful despite the challenges ahead? Because few things more convincingly highlight God's power and grace than His act of compassionately eliminating, at least for a while, Kim's memory of the accident and her suffering. She doesn't remember anything about the accident, starting from about two hours before it occurred until about two weeks later. She has no recollection whatsoever of those tortuous two weeks. Only a gracious God would create us in such a way that people such as Kim can be spared such agony. Surely, only God is wise enough to have created a shut-off switch in our mind that is automatically activated after we've endured more than we can bear.

After your mother was discharged from in-patient rehab at the Valley, we quickly felt the urge to re-engage with life. For several months, our lives had been a surreal circus of medical mayhem. We were desperate for a taste of "normalcy," which meant anything that resembled what we envisioned we would be doing were it not for the accident. I could sense the Dragon's desire to redefine our lives based on its terms, not ours, so I was very determined to resist letting the Dragon dictate every aspect of our lives: what we did and how we did it.

We had to be on guard against the temptation to consciously fight against the Dragon because doing so would have pulled us into the kind of engagement it desired: one in which my Tormentor – not us – defined the terms of our existence. A determined and dedicated confrontation is exactly what the Dragon desired. If it could not defeat us quickly, then it sought to do so slowly by separating us from everything except itself. Quite simply, if we gave the Dragon an inch, it would take a mile...then it would take our lives.

The Dragon tried to manipulate us through two sinister deceptions: one, that it didn't exist at all; and two, that should we indeed discover its existence, we could defeat it easily on our own. The more we allowed the Dragon to capture the focus of our attention, the less we were able to focus on God. If we kept our focus and attention on God and surrendered our concerns to Him, then He assumed the battle for us.

OCTOBER 10, 2003

GETTING ABOUT

Kim is getting better all the time. I think her arm strength, certainly, is greater than even before the accident. Her legs are also getting stronger, especially her right. Her left leg is also improving; it's just more "deliberate" than her right leg. Kim is now doing more and more things independently that previously required someone else's assistance. She is also registering for a driving class that will enable her to drive an adapted vehicle. This process takes a long time, and I suspect that she'll be walking by the time her

number is called. Kim's desire for independent living is what's driving all this. I love it. And I love her.

Kim and I are heading out tonight for dinner and a movie – a
real date! It is great to get out and be a part of the world, where
elements of both darkness and light co-exist. We cannot always
prevent the darkness from appearing, but it is nice to push ourselves toward the light. It's wonderful to feel like we have regained
a little control in how we navigate.

Your mother was incredibly dedicated in her physical therapy
and general rehabilitation. She was remarkable. Her schedule was
so demanding that I often wondered which one of us would be the
first to faint from exhaustion: your mother from doing it all or me
from watching her.

I remember accompanying her to a physical therapy session and
watching her navigate some of her first steps using the parallel bars.
The first thing she did was to get mentally prepared. She had to get
her mind focused on creating a positive attitude and put herself in a
"zone" in which she visualized success. As she pushed up out of her
wheelchair, using both arms and legs, I saw her quiet determination
become fixated on only one thing: moving her legs.

Initially, your mother had to look down at her legs in order to
verify what she was doing. She had so little sensation in her feet
and legs that she couldn't tell where they were without seeing them.
Also, focusing her eyes on her legs aided her determination. The
first few steps were painful and painfully slow. They were actually
less steps than they were weight shifts on the parallel bars, like the
way a gymnast would use her arms to maneuver across the same
bars. Your mother's legs didn't want to move, so she would push
herself up with her arms so that she could get just a little higher on

the parallel bars and then, was able to move her legs by swinging her hips during the momentary weight shift off her legs that her arms had created.

That was how your mother started to walk again. Very slowly, deliberately, and painfully, she swung her legs forward from her helps. Her legs didn't know how to do it on their own, so she had to teach them any way she could. Her courage and determination were inspiring.

Re-engaging for us meant getting back to living a life that was full of the richness of normalcy…and not taking it for granted. To engage in life deeply and meaningfully. Life didn't need to be profound, but rather, it had to be purposefully joined with the things that gave us the greatest joy. The simple things were usually where we found them. Children, of course, embodied the purest meaning of such joy.

We all went out for dinner one night near Stanford University, and you ran laps around the patio we were seated on. You were particularly enthusiastic about a table of young men, probably recent graduates, a couple of whom were amusing you with a game of "peek-a-boo." You suddenly came running over next to my chair and whispered enthusiastically, "I LOVE guys!" I raised my eyebrows and nodded somewhat patronizingly as if to disguise my dismay that this was all happening way too fast.

You nodded back and said, "Yep. They're sooo sneaky. That's why I'm so sneaky, too!" Then you took off and ran around the patio again, re-engaging the boys with your charm. I looked over at your mother, who smiled sympathetically. All I could think was: Please, please; let it stay this simple and innocent.

OCT 14, 2003

RE-ENGAGEMENT

Kim and I celebrated our wedding anniversary yesterday. We went out to a wonderful restaurant in Woodside, California called "The Village Pub." We had a night by ourselves as my parents stayed in and babysat Olivia. This was our first anniversary since the accident. It was a little auspicious because it also came the day after the one-year anniversary of the accident. Last night was a special night because I asked Kim to marry me again. I proposed, and she accepted.

I re-proposed because I wanted Kim to know that I still loved her. I wanted to assure her that we were going to stay together, no matter what. I wanted us to be a family, and not another statistic in the casualty column. I wanted our marriage and life together to be resilient and to stand up to adversity...even when life's events had forced us to sit down.

The condition, however, was that we change our anniversary date. I hated having to share our anniversary with the dark, looming cloud that represented a day that had brought into our lives such pain, disruption, and disconnectedness. I hated having to share our anniversary with a day in which the Dragon entered our lives. The accident had taken so much already; I couldn't bear the thought of it taking our wedding anniversary as well.

We decided right then and there that we would extend our re-engagement to the other parts of our lives, as well. We were not going to let the Dragon influence what we did or how we lived. We were going to re-engage in life to the very best of our abilities. We had now recovered enough, we were strong enough, and we were committed enough to live with gusto, not sorrow. We were finally at a place where we could look forward and start to re-engage and re-connect.

MIND CHATTER

Before the accident, I had a tortured relationship with sleep. Following the wreck, however, I was usually so tired that I had no difficulty falling asleep. Nevertheless, every now and then, my Tormentor stirred up a special brew that gently swirled in my stomach, causing an acidic reaction that forced every concern that I had buried to come bubbling up to the front of my brain. These tiny bubbles agitated my stream of consciousness and made it flow more rapidly than it ordinarily desired. My stream then started talking with my mind. It was less like chatter and more like gurgling, bubbling babble.

So what tasty little undigested morsels of concern did my Tormentor stir up for me? My mind gurgled and babbled along...

I would think about the fact that your mother could drive by herself. It was an amazing breakthrough in regaining some independence. She visualized herself as a "pilot" instead of a "driver." What a great confidence-building image! The van had great technology... more gadgetry than most Formula One racing cars. But I wondered what would happen if something broke down when she was alone? Would she be stranded? The stupid battery died all the time. I thought that your mother's sense of independence would be dashed if she couldn't trust the van to be dependable. Furthermore, operating that thing could be challenging. The van was very HEAVY. It needed a lot of time to slow down. And it had the maneuverability of a Zamboni.

I then thought about you growing up. You were learning to bounce on chairs and couches and beds. Okay, you were a kid. I used to love bouncing like that as well, when I was a kid. But I was worried sick about an injury if you fell and hit your head or neck. The thought of you becoming paralyzed was devastating. I wouldn't have been able to deal with it. I think your mother and I both would have died from broken hearts.

DEC 29, 2003

JOYFUL, JOYFUL

Last year at this time, we were very joyful because Kim was coming home from the hospital – permanently. This year, we had a chance to reflect on the enormous, positive progress that we have made in the past 12 months. It has been fairly dramatic, and it heightens our sense of awe and joy. Kim continues to get stronger and stronger. She has walked what seems like miles with the walker over the past few weeks. While it is still very demanding physically, it doesn't exhaust her quite like it used to. Her stamina is amazing.

Even though she is still in her wheelchair, Kim is now basically independent. She will be even more so, when we get around to ordering an adapted minivan. Of course, she continues to make progress toward her goal of ditching the chair entirely. We both remain very hopeful and optimistic. We also realize that none of our progress would have been possible without the love and support of our family and friends. I know I've said this before, but it is very humbling to be surrounded by such wonderful people and to be the beneficiaries of their kindness.

KEEPING STEPS AHEAD

"Steps Ahead" was one of my favorite concepts and it was also one of my favorite Jazz bands. Everything these guys did was classic. Your mother, as you should now realize, was also a classic. She continued to amaze me every day. Often, it was usually in the subtle ways that she demonstrated her courage, commitment, or quiet determination. Sometimes, however, she just couldn't help herself, and she knocked the cover off the ball.

John Wooden, the legendary UCLA basketball coach, urged his players to keep pushing because they were either getting better or they were getting worse. Quite simply, none of us can stay at the same level, regardless of how strong or weak we may be. It's the idea behind the notion of "constant improvement." Your mother was definitely getting stronger, and the idea of staying in the same place – stagnation – was abhorrent to her. "Steps ahead" was both catchy and appropriately inspirational.

Your mother maintained a strenuous physical therapy regimen that included weights, a recumbent bike, and walking. One of her greatest tricks was to tackle stairs. Yes, stairs. Your mother's adaptive physical education coach, Mary Bennett, was incredibly supportive in helping her reach higher levels. Your mother's desire to push even harder coincided with an invitation from our friend Ann Clarke to attend her birthday party at her new home in San Francisco. Ann's home, of course, was on the second floor of an older building...one without an elevator. Your mother heartily accepted the challenge.

After a couple weeks of training, we arrived at the big day and the challenge of taking on real stairs (not simulated ones) in the real world – not in a controlled setting. We were excited...and also incredibly nervous.

As usual, nothing was exactly how we had envisioned it. First, each step was much taller than what your mother had practiced on. Second, there were a few more steps in Ann's building than we had thought. Like...about ten more. Plus, there were two switchbacks — it was not a straight climb. We couldn't turn back, so it was onward and upward.

It was not the easiest thing we had done, but certainly not the most difficult either. We needed a little help, but we eventually made it. It was an incredible accomplishment worthy of thanks and celebration. It also gave us an even greater appreciation for basic freedom and independence.

RE-ENGAGEMENT REDUX

At first, I thought that moving our anniversary date away from the accident date was a good idea. It enabled us to celebrate and commemorate our wedding without the shadow of the accident looming over our heads. As I began to reflect on this, however, I began to be resentful that the accident had, again, been able to dictate certain parts of our lives and had caused us to change the things that mattered most to us in order to accommodate the intrusion that it had created. From the outset, we had been determined to try to not let the accident dictate how our lives would be lived. I suddenly realized that, by changing our anniversary date, I had violated that very goal.

Your mother and I had been very deliberate in choosing our wedding date. It was a beautiful time of year, when autumn is in full bloom and nature seems so crisp and alive. Our wedding date, in October, is also a time that we identified with the harvest, a time of celebration in which the gifts of God's earth are held up with a reverence that is unique to the season and those who work the land for their livelihood. For farmers and cultivators, harvest season is sacred. Our wedding date was just as important and sacred to us. Changing its date to accommodate the accident – to appease the Dragon – was not the answer. It was a capitulation and a thinly veiled admission of defeat.

Therefore, I decided that we could still re-commit ourselves in our marriage, but that we would keep our original wedding date. The accident had taken too much already; it didn't deserve to take the things that were precious and dear to us. The things that we still had control over were the things I was determined to not let the Dragon slither in and steal away.

CHAPTER NINETEEN

BETRAYAL

Faith in anything can only be trusted if it's put to the test.

I N THE MIDST OF THE CHAOS surrounding my battles with the System was the constant joy of your mother's steady recovery. She worked incredibly hard every day trying to regain her strength and rediscover even the tiniest movement. Your mother was slowly and painfully reconnecting with her body. Ironically, as she was reconnecting with her body, I seemed to be growing increasingly disconnected from my mind. Where had my mind gone? I was nowhere near it. I wanted to find one. Though sometimes I feared it. Whatever mind I had seemed to have a reaction speed that was inexcusably slow, as you will see.

MONEY CHANGES EVERYTHING

When people heard about our accident, their outpouring of love and support was incredible and touched us deeply. The question many asked was, "What can we do to help?"

Unfortunately, in those initial first few weeks, I was in no condition to respond. I was in and out of hospitals looking after your mother and getting treatment for my own injuries. I was further incapacitated by the insidious combination of narcotics and anxiety-coaxed adrenaline. The truth was, however, that I had no idea what people could do to help. I had no idea what needed to be done, what could be done, what we would have to do or would want to have done for us. I had no earthly clue. I had no idea what to ask for, so I asked for nothing.

Quite early on, someone suggested that we might need some money. "Perhaps," I responded, "but I haven't given it much thought. I've been focused on family health and survival issues."

That was a lie. I didn't want to contemplate money because it loomed as a big, unknown, and potentially scary consideration. We were not poor by any means, but I didn't need to build a spreadsheet to realize that our accident would be more than a simple financial "inconvenience." I didn't know exactly how much of an inconvenience it would be, but I had a feeling it might border on "disruptive."

In response, however, your Uncle Barry took the initiative to set up a dedicated fund at his local bank in Denver. After he set up the fund, he informed our network of friends and family of its existence and gave instructions on how to make contributions. He was very thorough in providing all the relevant information including address, account, and routing numbers. He even mentioned that the account had been established as a charitable trust, thereby enabling donors to receive potential tax benefits.

Except for a couple of small withdrawals, we left the money alone that had been contributed to the "Olivia and Kimberly Fund." The money in the fund came from the generosity of family, friends, colleagues, and complete strangers, who had all made loving contributions. Your mother and I felt that we should use the money in a meaningful way, something that would tangibly and significantly make an impact on our lives and which, without those funds, we might not have been able to procure.

We decided that an adapted minivan would be an ideal use of the proceeds. Such vehicles dramatically increased the quality of life for thousands of disabled people. Adapted vehicles helped make the outside world more accessible and fostered a greater sense of independence and self-sufficiency for those fortunate enough to have them.

Such vans, however, were not inexpensive. They had to be modified significantly in order for a disabled person to operate them independently. The hand controls used to drive the vehicle were fairly simple and inexpensive. The real cost, however, was in the sophisticated electronic and hydraulic systems that served to minimize the difficulties of entry and exit for someone in a wheelchair.

Before we pierced the veil, your mother and I held minivans with about as much regard as soap operas, stale bread, flat beer, and thirsty mosquitoes. My casual research had indicated beyond question that the absolute worst, most aggressive drivers on the road all drove minivans. This seemed to contradict their image as the ultimate family vehicle. I then surmised that all these suburbanite minivan drivers suffered from massive road rage because they were all so pissed off at having to drive minivans.

Your mother and I, city snobs that we were, vowed that we would never drive a minivan. We considered it the ultimate capitulation. As a guy, I considered it to be the white flag of manhood, akin to voluntary castration.

After we pierced the veil, however, our views changed on many things, including minivans. In our new state, we knew that a minivan would be a practical necessity. Therefore, we decided that an adapted minivan would be the perfect way in which to use the money from the Fund. We figured it would be a fitting reminder of the incredibly generous support we had received. We shared our intentions with everyone, including Barry.

Nevertheless, the road toward getting such a van was long and challenging. First of all, your mother needed to maintain her rehabilitation program in order to rebuild her strength and learn how to adapt in her new body. This required several more months of strenuous physical therapy because her body had not yet stabilized from the shock of its injury. She needed to be strong, stable, and coordinated enough to drive. It became a goal on which we set our sights, but it was still a long way off.

Therefore, we let the funds remain in the bank in Denver for several months. We were busy trying to rebuild our lives. Getting physically stronger, learning how to adjust in a new body, getting back to work, looking for a new home, and on, and on, and on.

I estimated that the money available in the Fund would not cover the entire cost of the van, but it would certainly help. Besides, even if the Fund only amounted to $2, this was the type of thing for which it was intended. Therefore, I finally emailed your Uncle Barry that we were now ready to buy the van and could he please initiate a wire transfer. He responded a couple of days later, writing that the funds were not available because he had incurred some unforeseen expenses and had needed to borrow the money. But that he could get it to us shortly. Ooohhhh. My stomach sank, and I felt a familiar pit return.

I was outraged, and I was numb. I couldn't believe this. What the hell?! I didn't know how to respond or react. So I emailed him back indicating that I understood and that I didn't need the money immediately, but preferably within the next couple of weeks. So I waited for what seemed like forever.

I then got an email from Barry declaring that the money would be coming "soon." Then another email a few days later indicating that the refinancing of his house was taking longer than expected. This was not welcome news, and I could see this was spiraling to nowhere. I finally broke the news to your mother, who, naturally, went completely ballistic.

Barry's betrayal was unbelievable. The money in the Fund that he had stolen did not even come from your mother and me; it had been given to us by other people for our benefit...and yours. It was not just an act of theft against us; it was a theft against them. It was a violation of their goodwill and generosity. It made me sick with shame and embarrassment. I was embarrassed for my family and for the fact that the kindness of so many people who had lovingly contributed money had been abused and violated.

What I felt most acutely, however, was the shame I felt from the inadvertent complicity of my benign neglect that resulted in everything becoming far worse than it had to be. I was ashamed that I let my knowledge of the situation linger for as long as I did before revealing it to your mother.

Once I told your mother, of course, her anger and fury quickly ignited my own sense of moral outrage. I asked to see complete bank statements. When they arrived, it became obvious that, amazingly, Barry had started making withdrawals only two months after he had opened the account. If that weren't bad enough, he had been sending out updates to our email group, encouraging people to make donations.

I had been so eager to attend Barry's wedding and reconnect with him because I had been thrilled that he was apparently getting his life together and emerging as a competent citizen in society. We went to see him and celebrate with him and for him. Then he did this?! I was blown away. It was as if the car that had hit us came back at me again, except this time, the force of the impact launched me out of the back window. I flew through air, somersaulting backwards in time for decades, way past all my sensibilities and into a world of utter madness. I could sense my Tormentor delighting in the fact that this was going to test my faith yet again, in ways I had never considered.

When Barry's betrayal finally hit me, it was like the steering column in our car had penetrated the air bag, shattered my rib cage and gone right through my heart. I had welcomed him home like my Prodigal Brother and let him back into my life fully and completely. I had trusted him, again. But Barry charmed better than a drug-addicted Vaudeville vixen capable of enchanting any chump who had the money to secure a quick fix. He would have shown more integrity had he stabbed me in the back with a tire iron.

The viciousness of Barry's betrayal exposed another violation of trust. It made me look inward and confront my own hideous betrayal of your mother. It exposed with horrifying clarity that I had been shielding your mother from much that was going on in my life and ours. I was keeping too much to myself and preventing her from being part of my life, from sharing with her what I was going through as much as she was sharing with me what she was enduring. I didn't realize that she was strong enough to take it. I selfishly refused to admit, yet again, that I was not strong enough to carry it alone. I felt ashamed and unworthy of your mother's love and trust.

I should have told your mother immediately about your uncle's malfeasance. By keeping it in, I let it get out of hand. Of course, it was easy to justify my actions because I was trying to protect your mother from yet another rotten element brought on by the accident, which had already caused profound anguish and sorrow. She had paid such a heavy toll that I tried to protect her from things that I thought would reignite the drama of her ordeal and trigger her nerve pain. I didn't want to add to her already considerable burden by exposing her unnecessarily to things that I thought I could contend with by myself.

But I was wrong. As a result, your mother suffered, I suffered, Barry suffered, and our families suffered. Furthermore, I set a bad example of what effective, compassionate leadership should be. It was completely opposite of what I would want to exhibit for you and how I would want you to conduct yourself.

In my world, trust was something that was gained after playing catch with someone for a while. That person would say, do and throw things our way. How we perceived the velocity, spin and intention of what he or she threw us determined the degree of trust we would extend and, in gauging subsequent throws, whether we should step forward with eager anticipation, step aside, or duck.

When we took a leap of faith and established a baseline of trust, we assumed that every ongoing interaction with that person would strengthen and build upon that foundation. When our trust was broken, however, we felt violated not only by that person, but also by ourselves because we felt our sense of judgment had been faulty, if not fraudulent. Betrayal raised suspicion regarding every other significant decision that involved discernment or intuition. Betrayal caused concern over every assessment of individual character, starting with our own. And betrayal had the potential to crumble the foundation of everything in our lives to which we ascribed value. Betrayal could cause the very things we once held most dear to become virtually worthless.

In betrayal's wake, we were left empty, longing, and lacking. We felt completely alone and were desperate to cling to anything, even to the shadows of our departed beliefs, which, on the way out, were speechless in their own defense.

As I've said before, the cost of waiting can be huge.

FORGIVENESS AND MOVING ON

Your Uncle Barry's malfeasance was extremely challenging. While Barry said that he was sorry he got caught, he never apologized for his theft, lies, and total avoidance of responsibility. It would have been nice to receive an apology, and in truth, I waited for one as if I were entitled to it, like a child who might play the lottery for the first time. I felt he owed us at least an apology. Of course, Barry didn't feel that way.

While waiting for Barry's apology, my heart quietly hardened to him and his family, and it grew heavier and harder as time went on. It became one of those unresolved issues that accumulated dust the longer it stayed on the shelf. Like stale bread, it just sat there in plain view, getting harder and crustier. And one wanted to touch it. The last thing I needed or wanted in my life was accumulated, unresolved, crusty issues. They may have been small and relatively insignificant individually, but collectively they added up to a weighty burden that would only compound negative interest over time and result in moral bankruptcy or bad karma.

If I was going to get past this, I realized that I needed to initiate forgiveness of Barry instead of waiting for him to apologize or ask for forgiveness. In so doing, of course, I realized that I also needed to seek his forgiveness as well. I may have been justified in all my actions, but they were still hurtful to him.

On the surface, my intent in forgiving Barry was to lighten the load for each of us. But the truth is that if I was going to truly move past this issue, I needed to release Barry from liability and overcome the anger I felt toward him with a demonstration of God's love, if not my own. I realized that God would hold me accountable if I failed to forgive Barry and continued to harbor resentment, no matter how deeply buried or how seemingly justifiable. Resentment from my hardened heart could easily give birth to the seeds of hatred. My Tormentor may have wanted this for me; but God did not. Grace, I realized, applied equally to Barry as much as it did to me.

Therefore, it didn't really matter that Barry never responded in kind. Yes, he wrote back and apologized for getting caught but not for his actions. And he was willing to accept my apologies and forgiveness, but he didn't offer his own in turn. Ultimately, I realized that it didn't matter. What I do know is that the act of offering Barry my forgiveness held the Dragon at bay and forced it to eat a loaf of crusty bread.

Forgiveness helped usher in redemption. Forgiveness was how we moved on and made peace with others and with ourselves. I learned a great deal about my own capacity to forgive during the years following our accident. It was a complex issue that forced me to get completely naked in front of the ultimate, illuminating question of whom I was truly serving: God or myself.

CHAPTER TWENTY

FINDING THE FALL LINE

If you don't know where you're going, any road will take you there.

THE FALL LINE WAS THE PATH OF LEAST RESISTANCE. We used to refer to it while traversing down a ski slope so that we would expend minimal effort and avoid unnecessary turns and bumps. But the term applied equally to how we traversed through life's obstacles. Because some of the challenges are new and appear difficult, there is a tendency to make life harder than it needs to be. Even if we find the Fall Line, or the path of least resistance, most people will quickly get discouraged and give up because the hardest part is at the top, at the very beginning. The first part is the steepest.

In life as in skiing, it usually helped to observe others go first to see the line that they took and, accordingly, learn from it. Whenever possible, we avoided many mistakes by first observing – or at least asking questions – before jumping onto a new trail.

Falling down and failing is okay, provided you get up and acknowledge what didn't work. Next time, you'll find the path easier, and you'll be more confident on it. I began to ski as a young child, and I remember one of the first things I learned was how to fall. Learning how to fall was important because it helped minimize the fear and embarrassment of falling. It made me a less inhibited skier. I taught you the same thing on skis, but I'm not sure I adequately prepared you for how to fall in life. I didn't fully know how to force you to fall, and I probably didn't allow you to fall often enough.

Understandably, you got angry with me on those occasions when I could have prevented you from falling but didn't. There was no way for you to understand – certainly then and perhaps even now – that getting up from your falls was far more important for you than avoiding any momentary pain, grievance or embarrassment they may have caused. I could teach you how to fall in certain sports, but you had to learn it yourself in the game of life.

JANUARY 19, 2004

ANGELS TAKE THEMSELVES LIGHTLY

We are firm believers that angels are all around us, all the time. I believe some of them work very consciously on God's behalf; working for Him – full time, all the time – as He directs and instructs. Others are used more sparingly (perhaps only once) and might not even be aware consciously that God is using them as messengers in specific situations. Angels serve as conduits that connect those they contact with both the exact answer to a specific question as well as a very clear sign that God is present, all-knowing, and all-powerful. He is also very creative in His delivery methods.

We have had scores of personal encounters and experiences. Since our accident, especially, we have been highly sensitive to how angels work in our lives. Ideally, I should chronicle these incidents and share them liberally with others. But, as you can tell from my increasing absent or tardy updates and responses, I may not be the most qualified or reliable person to spread the news. Besides, there are plenty of fine books that detail such encounters. Regardless, it is only important that we recognize them, be grateful, and acknowledge from whom they came.

One such incident merits special mention. Kim has always loved alpine skiing. When we first learned that she was pregnant with Olivia, one of the joyful aspirations we shared was our desire to get Olivia on skis early in life and enjoy as a family all the wonders of winter, especially skiing together as a family. The accident, of course, placed some obvious challenges in front of realizing those aspirations.

In our new world since the accident, however, we have an opportunity to learn about things we never knew existed. Navigating in this world requires trust, courage and reliance on unfamiliar people and resources. The wonderful thing about the friends we have is that so many have become our allies and advocates. Through them, we have a vastly extended network of eyes, ears, hands, and mouths to work on our behalf. Many of our friends are uncommonly bright, creative, and insightful. They think about opportunities we have not imagined or solutions we have yet to consider. Sometimes, we are too exhausted, drained, or tapped. Usually, however, those are just convenient excuses for not seeing or thinking at a higher level, where angels operate.

When it became obvious early on that skiing for Kim might look different from what she was accustomed, some of our friends quickly set out to explore this new world for us. The first thing we discovered is that there are indeed adaptive ski programs. Okay, where? Well, our friend Inga, an avid skier, learned that Alpine Meadows at Lake Tahoe has one of the better adaptive ski programs in the region. That was good to know. But we were still unclear about all the logistics: how to get started, what to bring, what to do, how it all works, etc. Sure, we could make some phone calls and gather all the appropriate info, but even with all that knowledge, we were still somewhat apprehensive. For a first-time experience like that, it is nice to have a guide, a shepherd. Someone who is familiar with both the physical and emotional terrain.

Sure enough, our friend Inga was outside her house at Lake Tahoe late last year when a piece of paper landed on her driveway. She had seen this paper fluttering in the wind and watched it land gently just a few feet in front of her. The deliberateness of the paper's landing caused her to look carefully at the paper instead of ball it up in disgust as we often do when an unwanted piece of litter intrudes on our domain.

As she observed the now landed and gated flying object, she noticed that it was no mere piece of paper but, rather, a brochure! Rather heavy to be carried on the wind. Interesting. Upon closer inspection, she saw that this brochure was for...of all things, the adaptive ski program at Alpine Meadows. Awesome! Coincidence...?

A few weeks later, Inga was at Squaw Valley Ski Resort when a fellow who called himself "the Candy Man" came around. All the regulars of the locker at Squaw had known the Candy Man for years because he was always handing out small candy bars of some variety. Inga innocently stopped him and asked him why he did this. He responded that after his early retirement, he thought spreading a little joy would be a small way to give something back. Candy was a small but tangible way to make a small gift to strangers. He then went on to say that he loved doling out goodies at Squaw, but that he really loved being the Candy Man over at Alpine Meadows, where there are more families and kids. Furthermore, the people on the adapted skis at Alpine are especially appreciative of his little acts of kindness. Hmmm, this was interesting.

Inga inquired further about the Candy Man's interaction with adapted skiers and if he knew anything about the program. Not only did he know something about the program, he was one of the instructors! He had been doing it for years and it was one of his great passions in life. He told her that he felt "called" to help out in that way and it had become his favorite form of "giving back."

Naturally, Inga got his business card and said she was going to give it to us. The Candy Man enthusiastically insisted that we contact him as soon we were ready to begin skiing again. Amazing! Coincidence? Hardly. There are no coincidences. The more I pay attention to the details of life, the more I realize that God's actions – either directly or through messengers – are anything but coincidental. Words such as "coincidence," "random," and "arbitrary" are the lexicon of those who have not believed enough to see God's divine plan.

FUN AND GAMES

For your mother and me, few things in life were as much fun and exhilarating as alpine skiing. Before the accident, we envisioned teaching you how to ski at an early age. We wanted you to develop good fundamental skills early, but it was a conveniently self-serving excuse that enabled your mother and me to go skiing as well. After the accident, however, we were not sure if we would ever be able to ski together as a family. We knew we could physically, of course. But would either of us be able to handle it emotionally? Your mother had been such a good skier: elegant, graceful, strong, and courageous. She was way better than I was. We knew that getting back on the mountain would be a great test of our faith and determination to keep moving forward.

As you may have surmised, your mother and I were big fans of anything Italian. We just loved the language, culture, cuisine, and lifestyle. We even loved the things that should have driven us nuts – like the periodic train strikes, which we found peculiar and, yet, somehow or innocently endearing.

We were thrilled when we heard that the 2006 Winter Olympic Games had been awarded to Italy. We schemed and dreamed of going to Torino and becoming Italian for a week or two. Then we got pregnant with you, which altered our thinking, but not our intentions. Then the accident happened, which closed the door on our little Torino fantasy.

As the Olympic Games drew nearer, we began to reminisce about our involvement in winter sports. I used to be a competitive ice hockey player, and we both loved to ski. We had actually made our first "connection" with each while on a church group ski trip. Skiing was a huge part of our shared lives. We would have skied a lot more had my career been more accommodating, but we skied whenever I had some visibility in my schedule that didn't involve business travel.

Your mother was by far the better skier. She had a certain grace and speed that were mesmerizing and of which I was slightly jealous. She went down the mountain with such ease that I always thought she had special skis or, better yet, special guidance from angels. She seemed to just float down the hill, as if on a cloud.

I, on the other hand, always seemed to be fighting the mountain. My hockey training somehow made me feel obliged to attack the mountain and exert my influence on it. I worked hard at my turns and I always seemed to force them at awkward apexes, instead of where the fall line of the mountain wanted to lead me. (Which was, fittingly, an appropriate analogy to my faith journey.) Your mother worked with me and pushed me to work with the mountain, not against it. Skiing got us excited about nature and about God and about being alive. We found that God was both revealed and readily accessible in the midst of His wintry creation. It was rejuvenating.

After the accident, life was about moving forward. With each other and with God. We could not move forward alone, because it would be impossible to tell if our movement alone was relative or absolute. Whatever movement we achieved was not validated if it had been made alone. We needed the company of others to validate, if not verify, our very existence. The same, of course, was true of love. It could not be achieved alone.

OUR OLYMPIC MOMENT

Your mother was determined to get back to the mountains and try adaptive skiing ever since she heard about it from our friend Inga. We seized the moment on one particular holiday weekend. We loaded up the van and set out for Lake Tahoe on a Thursday night. The drive took about six hours but included a stop for dinner. We not only avoided much of the weekend traffic, but also missed a big snowstorm that dropped about a foot of snow on Friday. Others who left the Bay Area on Friday night needed up to 12 hours to get to Lake Tahoe.

As usual, you and I got up early the next morning and hit the breakfast room. You were in need of chocolate milk, and I was in need of coffee (I was always in need of coffee). I normally loved such times when you and I got to have a quiet time together over breakfast. Often, however, my time with you was interrupted or distracted by a conference call that I needed to be on.

More challenging on this particular day was that our breakfast was not in the quiet of our house as usual but in restaurant that we had to share with others. It was rustic and charming and overlooked a beautiful, flowing river. Snow was falling like crazy, clinging to pine trees and piling up on the river rocks like giant, fluffy snow cones. It was the kind of idyllic scene that arrested the attention of any sane person and demanded that one cease all other activities to appreciate and respect the rare, serene beauty of the moment.

Of course, because I only pretended to be sane, such rules did not apply to me. Friday was still a workday, and I needed to be on a conference call. Not only was I unable to wholly savor the beauty all around me, but I was also disturbing all the others around me by my reckless phone manners. I was the obnoxious guy with the loud voice and a bad phone connection. Plus, I was running after you and trying to get some breakfast into you...hoping that providing you with a good breakfast would offset the obvious neglect I was showing you. You were cute but still required a little parental involvement for your basic necessities.

From a distance, such things are always comical. Picture, if you will: a stressed-out dad trying repeatedly to get his child's hot chocolate just right, while attempting to conduct business on a phone with a bad connection between huge gulps of desperately needed coffee that was annoyingly weak, and having to give chase to the child who periodically took flight out of the restaurant due to boredom, neglect, embarrassment, or desperation.

We survived that small episode, though the proverbial egg on my face came in the form of chocolate milk, Cheerios, bananas and the requisite brown stains from some beverage masquerading as coffee. Despite bumbling early on, this was going to be special day. We were going to go skiing! This was our Olympic Event!

Even on the best days, it took a while for all of us to get ready and out the door. I usually could not even think about shaving or getting dressed before my eighth cup of coffee. Back then, I had to feed and dress you and then help your mother with some minor things. We usually needed about two hours, though admittedly, half of that time was consumed by my trips to the coffee machine.

On a ski day, however, we got creative when it came to getting ourselves ready. Ski clothes were cumbersome. They were even more cumbersome when we had forgotten how the darn things were supposed to go on, such as the order of things and their direction. Meanwhile, you got upset because you wanted to go skiing in your princess outfit and were distraught that you couldn't find it. You didn't understand why we hadn't packed it, and you were putting on a pout that caused my blood pressure to rise rapidly and, accordingly, made me realize that I'd had way too much coffee. You suggested, rather forcefully, that you could instead ski in your pajamas or maybe just your underwear.

We eventually got to the adaptive ski program, where your mother got fitted with a mono ski and prepared for a lesson. Alpine's Adaptive Ski Program was among the oldest and most respected programs dedicated to helping people with disabilities (physical and developmental) get on skis and out on the mountain. It was a wonderful program staffed solely by trained volunteers.

To be sure, your mother was a little anxious. She had always been a good skier, but this would be different. She wondered how it would compare with the sensation of skiing as she used to know it. The thought of contrasting a new experience in a compromised body with one she had so dearly loved in her previous state was bitter sweet. More important, she wondered if she could she do it, physically.

Nevertheless, it was a blessing just to be in the snow and on the mountain. We praised God we got even that far. Furthermore, we would all be skiing together. You were making your debut, and I managed to squeeze my feet into a pair of boots so that I could carve up the bunny slope like the slalom champion portrayed in my humble imagination.

Your mother, of course, was astonishing on the slopes. She mastered her adaptive ski sled in no time and was quickly, as usual, going down the hill faster than me. It was an incredible feeling of independence for her and me. It was great for her to know that she could do it; it was great for me to realize just how truly capable she was.

Another great benefit was that your mother really liked skiing like this. Sure, it was different from skiing with boards on her feet, but on a sled, she was so much closer to the snow. She could experience the snow, wind, and sound that much more intensely…and she got to go really fast!

Life and love were synonymous whenever God was present. Not surprisingly, when we went skiing in the mountains, we found ourselves closer to God. His love was magnified and came more fully alive. And when we were going fast on skis, our hearts also beat just a bit faster. At the time, I assumed that the heightened exhilaration was because we were chasing God. I now know that it was because we were chasing each other.

For us, traveling on the fall line was a new way of life. It meant focusing on what mattered most and not getting attached to appealing distractions. It sometimes meant removing clutter that got in the way, even if the clutter was composed of memories, mementos, or reminders of things we once held dear. It meant removing the peripheral fat of what we really wanted or needed so that we could firmly embrace their irreducible minimums. It meant figuring out the most efficient route to joy and, along the way, how to best navigate the System while keeping the Dragon at bay.

Our Olympic moment – when we were able to get back on skis and reconnect with the mountain – was a moment of pure joy. It made us feel as light and carefree, as if the sun had melted away our burdens, which were then absorbed by the snow, for which they were of no consequence. Being on skis – just getting on skis – was incredibly empowering. It was intoxicating: it felt so good that we wanted the feeling to last forever. I started thinking about the possibility of living in ski country. I asked myself: Why shouldn't we just move to the mountains? Why don't we just give up the rat race and move somewhere that sings to our souls and yet makes my Tormentor squirm? I started to like the idea even more as I began to figure that it would likely be less expensive for us to live in the mountains than in the Bay Area. Gee, more fun, less stress, less expensive...' what's wrong with this picture?

Then I started to sober up. My mind began to succumb to doubt as it cycled through all the obstacles we might come across if we really were to move: What about work? What on earth would I do to make a living? What about friends? What about school for Olivia? What about finding an appropriate house and making it accessible? What about rehabilitation therapy and special medical care for Kim? What about church?

We didn't really know anyone up in the mountains, and as much as I liked the idea of being in nature – amidst the invigorating crisp, clean air, close to skiing and God's visible handiwork, I started to realize that the allure that moving there held for me was because it represented an escape from wherever we currently were. Or, more appropriately: wherever I was. Escaping to live in the mountains would end up being more stressful than whatever I was trying to elude.

As I now reflect on that decision, which seemed so long ago, it stands out as one of those classic inner confrontations between head and heart. My heart sought joy and constant communion with God.

My head was determined to lead me down roads that appeared to proclaim victory against my Tormentor. My head was a soldier that wanted us to march victorious and receive a hero's welcome, like in Paris when the French were liberated from the Nazis. My heart could have cared less about a demonstrable victory; it just wanted to be at peace.

Nevertheless, whereas my heart was often defenseless to the onslaughts of my Tormentor, my head was a steely protector and often savvy to the deceptions of the Trickster. Unfortunately, my head also tended to over-react and be so protective that my heart would practically suffocate from within the depths of its heavily fortified bunker. My head tried to protect my heart from being wounded; but my head also prevented my heart from being free. If my heart was able to express something through an air pipe from deep within its bunker, then my head was often quick to seal the pipe off, fearing that my Tormentor would thrust itself down the open pipe like some kind of heat-seeking, heart-stopping missile.

The problem with my head is that it became so vigilant in its quest to keep my Tormentor at bay that my mind rarely rested. Because my mind would wander, as would a stealthy field sentry on the lookout for signs of approaching trouble, there were numerous false sightings. As battle fatigue became a daily reality, my Tormentor, ever the Great Deceiver, was able to occasionally insert its own cleverly disguised thoughts such that they slipped past my mind, undetected. My head would then absorb these twisted, sordid thoughts as if they were its own. Therefore, I could not determine whether those "rational" thoughts about not moving to the mountains were my own or if they were, instead, served up by my Tormentor, who preferred that I be rational and trapped rather than joyful and free.

In my world, we tried all kinds of ways to manufacture Grace. We tried to somehow replicate it and, of course, even buy it. None of it worked: not the drugs, the consumption of food, toys, money, power, or fame. They all eventually deflated and became empty, lonely vessels. We finally realized that Grace came from God alone, who gave it freely. But the cost of acceptance was, for some in my world, too much to bear.

While God gave His grace freely, in order for us to accept it and hold onto it, we had to first unload and let go of what we treasured. Catching is easy, but letting go is hard. In my world, we were so possessive and childish in our understanding of ownership. We confused what we owned with what was merely on loan to us.

Someday, we will all be called to the Mother Ship, which doesn't accept baggage. Once aboard, we will have permanent Grace and joy. I take great comfort in knowing that when I am finally called, my Tormentor will not be granted a boarding pass. My Tormentor will be left behind to stew in the stench of its own halitosis and not on the leftovers from the table of my self-centeredness. Only then will my Tormentor cease to exist for me, finally disconnected from my very being.

Until then, I will do my little dance with my Tormentor, strangely thankful that its very presence has helped me lean on God more than I ever could have done otherwise. And we will travel down our new fall line. We'll do it as gracefully as we can but will usually stumble, roll, and flail about. We'll bounce over the bumps and curse the rough patches we thought we could have avoided. We'll be an odd sight, riding down the hill on our funky sleds.

Yet, we're all on the same hill. All of us. All we can do – with love and desperation – is to try to keep each other from falling off our crazy toboggans.

We are bound together with a strange assortment of hope on a string, sacrificial nails, bent metallic humor, and a joyful abundance of makeshift Band-Aids. Our seat cushions of faith are soft yet firm, but it's a challenge to keep them under us when we're being tossed about on our uncertain ride. They keep us grounded, so we cling to them as best we can. But we know we are on the right course, on the fall line, when we feel the joy of God's presence, which, of course, can be anywhere.

CHAPTER TWENTY-ONE

A BEACON

The heaviest part of baggage of what we leave behind.

A S WE TRAVELED ON OUR ROAD TO RECOVERY, your mother and
I became the beneficiaries of incredible kindness, warmth,
and generosity. At the very least, we owed a debt of gratitude to the
countless people who helped to ease the burden of our journey. Along
the way, we were able to connect with friends, both new and old, in
ways we were not expecting. Along the way, many of these people approached us believing that, somehow, we could help them. This was a
surprising and awkward realization for your mother and me. It left us
a little perplexed until we took an honest look at ourselves.

The accident and its aftermath stripped naked many of the
strengths as well as the defense systems that we had developed over
the years. We were wounded and, thus, vulnerable. Our faults,
failures and weaknesses were exposed for all to see. Furthermore,
these were all very transparent, within clear view, and we did little
to cover them up...though I tried mightily at times to keep a stiff
upper lip.

We did not have much to hide, and we had neither the strength
nor the patience to try to cover things up. Our sense of pride and

security had been broken and we had quit being modest after numerous hospital procedures involving pokes, prods, ill-fitting hospital gowns, and countless moments of being put in positions of potential embarrassment. The transparency and vulnerability that we had developed, therefore, provided for many people the elements of trust and safety that made us seem approachable. We became something of a safety beacon.

A long time ago, during the height of the great Internet Bubble of the late twentieth century, stories abounded of people who became overwhelmed with the suddenness of their acquired wealth. Therapists were overbooked with people seeking help from the stress that resulted from sudden huge financial windfalls. It seemed the common complaint was that many of these people felt somehow unqualified and that the responsibilities of managing such enormous riches overpowered their ability to respond appropriately, especially when compared to both how life used to be as well as the apparent randomness of being selected to receive such windfalls. In a word: people felt undeserving.

It was often how your mother and I felt following our accident. Our windfall was not of a financial or material kind; it was in the form of love, prayers and support from so many people. What made it truly amazing to us, and why it touched us so profoundly, was that our windfall was one giant collective gift of love from others, some of whom we barely knew.

The love and support that comprised our windfall had a depth and meaning to us that a dispassionate financial bonanza could not approximate. It truly amazed us that we should be the beneficiaries of such a generous windfall. And yes, it was very difficult to know how to respond appropriately because the windfall and what prompted it were indeed so different from how our lives used to be.

Our windfall was too great to hoard and keep for ourselves alone. We reasoned that if we shared it and spread it, it would grow to even greater proportions. We tried to re-circulate our windfall back into the general jet stream of good intentions. We felt that it if it were passed along to others then, at least indirectly, it would come back to those who had initiated it. It eventually became a self-perpetuating, self-sustaining, self-fulfilling windfall of emotional riches. Joy instead of despair or discouragement. At least that was our intent.

There was always a silver lining, if we looked hard enough. Sometimes, we did not have to look but, rather, wait. Waiting was definitely more challenging than looking, especially in my world, which suffered from attention deficit disorder and needed immediate gratification. Your mother and I, through our ordeal, acquired new definitions of "patience." But we still had to learn that all great things were worth waiting for. You, certainly, were a perfect example of that time-tested and re-tested principle.

One of the most obvious and tangible blessings I witnessed from waiting was the dramatic extent to which your mother recovered from her injuries. Immediately following our accident, our primary prayers were for her to regain the use of her arms and hands so that she could hold you and nurture you the way most mothers did. Many people who suffered spinal cord injuries at your mother's level did not regain full use of their arms and hands. We enlisted everyone we knew to pray on your mother's behalf so that she may regain some of her hand and arm functionality. Our prayers were heard...and answered.

Your mother worked incredibly hard every day and kept striving for more regained mobility. She continued to succeed, to get stronger, and to do more of the things she wanted to do or needed to do. Before we knew it, she was able to get dressed, cook, drive, and, yes, hug and hold you. She became way more independent anyone could have imagined. But what would you expect from a West Texas Testarossa?

Your mother's growing freedom from within the confines of Quadriplegia was directly correlated to her determination to work hard and to work with God. More than anyone I knew, your mother did not just invite God into her life, she yielded her life to Him. She let Him take over. Her independence was because of her dependence on God. Consequently, everyone who knew your mother was blessed because they got to bear witness to God working in her life.

By no means did we rejoice in our affliction, nor did we embrace it as some medal of bravery born from a battlefield. Instead, we came to the humble realization that while our affliction did not cause our weaknesses, it did reveal them. Therefore, we received our condition for what it was, with the hope and belief that through it, God would create in us new life. Perhaps it was this new life in us that others saw. Loving other people (as we had been so loved) allowed God to work through us so that He could be at work in them. Taken further, this concept raised a far deeper consideration, one that we would not have been prepared to answer – let alone acknowledge – before our accident:

Did we believe in God in order for Him to serve us?

Or for us to serve Him?

You may wonder how we found such blessings from such adversity. A pragmatic, secular answer lies in the realization that we were indeed very fortunate that we were not worse off. There was always someone in much worse condition, with far greater challenges, with much more intense and desperate suffering.

The more satisfying answer comes from the realization that God did not rescue us from our challenges; He rescued us in our challenges. God did not want us to suffer, but He allowed it because it enabled us to further rely, depend, and lean on Him. It allowed us to be closer to Him.

Although God did not perform mighty, headline-making miracles in our lives, we nevertheless prayed constantly that He would restore strength and feeling in your mother's legs so that she could walk. We prayed for the discovery of cures for spinal cord injuries to bring your mother and others like her back into the world of the freely mobile. We prayed for God to perform miracles. What He gave us, however, above all else, was His fellowship. He entered into our lives and stayed beside us. The comfort and assurance of His fellowship were greater than any miracle we might have otherwise hoped for.

We were once wayward travelers, not knowing that we were lost. But we got transformed into a beacon for other travelers like the ones we once were. This was possible only because of how God made all of us. Whatever pain or anguish our minds and bodies experienced was eclipsed by the gratitude our hearts remembered.

CHAPTER TWENTY-TWO

RECONNECTING

Grace cannot be manufactured, reformulated, or bought at a discount.

I THANK GOD EVERY DAY THAT YOU WERE NOT HURT in the accident. It seems like it was a million years ago, and I'm sometimes tempted to believe that it never happened. Then I wake up and confront the daily reminders, which conspire to disconnect me from the place we once shared. I have tried to shield you from many of the ways in which the accident has impacted us because I've wanted you to have as normal and happy a childhood as possible. Writing this enabled me to decompress, de-stress, and otherwise blow off steam. Please know that the frustrations I've expressed here or that you may have witnessed were not in any way caused by you.

I also wrote this because I wanted to leave you with some lasting impression (favorable I hope) should something happen to me before you were old enough for us to really know each other. Life is a gift, but it can be taken away at any moment. I did not want to wait for an appropriate time and take the chance that such a time may never come. And I certainly didn't want to wait so long that we were well into our role reversals: you not remembering that you ever drooled and me not remembering that I ever did not.

I hope you know – really know – how much you are loved. Your mother and I loved you even before you were born. Amazingly, God loves you even more. Never forget that.

When life gets hard (and it will) or when things don't make sense (and they won't) or when you are feeling sad and unappreciated (and you will), just remember that God loves you more than you can imagine. Your mother and I will always love you, but we know there will be times when we do things wrong or that you feel that we simply let you down. It will happen. We make mistakes and sometimes get distracted. We are human and fallible. God, however, never gets distracted.

When you endure hardship, know that it is for a reason. Any valuable tool or piece of equipment needs to be tested and pushed to its limits in the laboratory before it can be ready for service in the field. So it is with us. God is not testing you to see if you are worthy; He is preparing you for something greater than you can imagine. Just remember that when God starts something, He already knows how it is going to end.

You may think you are being used for something great and worthy, or you may think that what you do is inconsequential. The truth is that you may never find out while you are still alive. Your "great" endeavor may be a temporary flash, while your "inconsequential" work may evolve into one of the world's most important contributions…but long after your involvement.

The most important thing is that your hardship is really a means for you to draw closer to God. He may not protect you from your loss, but he'll guard you in it and through it. It is also entirely possible that while you are waiting for your hardship to pass or for your opportunity to arrive, who you become in the process may be more important than what you are waiting for.

Finally, it would please me greatly if others can somehow benefit from our experience. I certainly do not profess any particular wisdom or insights that will enhance people's lives. Nor do I presume that we, or our situation, are in any way unique. There are many more people with far greater challenges and adversities than ours. My guess is that such people would likely say something similar if they were to write such a book.

That is this: The key to everything – to surviving, coping with loss, adapting to changed realities, and managing to get by – is primarily an attitude that is defined by three words: Faith, Hope, and Love. And that is how we find and reconnect with joy – a peaceful, reassuring joy that can comes only from Faith, Hope and Love. That is all. If nothing else has touched your heart and sparked your mind, then I will consider my efforts worthwhile beyond measure.

Your mother and I endured significant physical and emotional pain. As you will someday learn, pain grinds away at your reserves and your resolve. But pain also brings a sense of joy when it helps you to recognize and be grateful for all the things you once took for granted. That sense of joy is deeper and more profound than any you'd known before piercing the veil. And it is the most tangible sign of being reconnected to the things that matter most.

Our journey has not been easy, but we never would have survived together without God's grace. Combined with His enduring strength, and the support of others, it is your mother's patient love and courage that enable us to keep reconnecting with joy. Again and again…and again.

*G*IL AHRENS HAS HELPED DOZ-
ENS OF BUSINESSES GROW,
change and evolve. As a business
executive for more than two decades, he has advised business
leaders and companies on working
through the challenges of both growth and adversity. Early in his
business career, he co-founded a consumer electronics company. He
then worked as a strategic planning executive in Japan for a large
global manufacturing company. He was most recently a Managing
Director of Investment Banking at J.P. Morgan.

Gil was born in Suffield, Connecticut and now resides in the
San Francisco Bay Area with his wife and young daughter. Together, they all succumb to the whims of Sparky, their domineering Jack
Russell Terrier, and Bella, a demur Scottish Terrier determined to
dominate every inanimate object.

He attends Menlo Park Presbyterian Church and was an elder at Calvary Presbyterian Church in San Francisco. He is on the board of directors at Abilities United, a non-profit in Palo Alto, California that helps champion those with developmental or physical challenges. Gil holds degrees from New York University and Boston University.

Gil is passionate about ice hockey, Formula 1 racing, University of Texas football, and good cigars…a vice he acknowledges freely.

Visit Gil Ahrens online at www.gilahrens.com

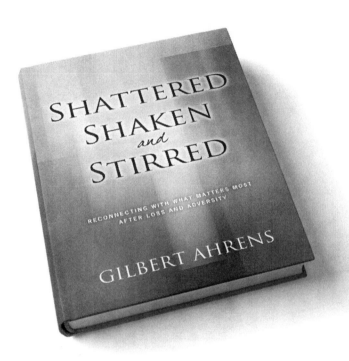

Additional copies of this book are available at

www.gilahrens.com

or Amazon.com

LaVergne, TN USA
13 January 2010
169961LV00002B/279/P